DEMOS

Demos is an independent think tank committed to radical thinking on the long-term problems facing the UK and other advanced industrial societies.

It aims to develop ideas – both theoretical and practical – to help shape the politics of the twenty first century, and to improve the breadth and quality of political debate.

Demos publishes books and a regular journal and undertakes substantial empirical and policy oriented research projects. Demos is a registered charity.

In all its work Demos brings together people from a wide range of backgrounds in business, academia, government, the voluntary sector and the media to share and cross-fertilise ideas and experiences.

For further information and
subscription details please contact:
Demos
9 Bridewell Place
London EC4V 6AP
Telephone: 0171 353 4479
Facsimile: 0171 353 4481
email: mail@demos.co.uk

Other publications available from Demos:

The rise of the social entrepreneur
A piece of the action: employee ownership, equity pay and the rise of the knowledge economy
Civic spirit: the big idea for a new political era
The return of the local

To order a publication or a free
catalogue please contact Demos

Civic
entrepreneurship

Charles Leadbeater and Sue Goss

DEMOS

in association with

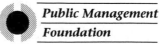

Public Management
Foundation

First published in 1998
Reprinted in 1999
by Demos
Panton House
25 Haymarket
London SW1Y 4EN
Tel: 0171 321 2200
Fax: 0171 321 2342
email: mail@demos.co.uk
© Demos 1998

ISBN 1 898309 39 6
Printed in Great Britain by BDW Associates
Design by Lindsay Nash

Contents

Acknowledgements

Most of the best ideas are borrowed and we borrowed the phrase civic entrepreneurship from an organisation called Collaborative Economics in Palo Alto, California. Collaborative Economics use the phrase civic entrepreneurship to describe the role of business leaders in creating public partnerships through the innovative Joint Venture Silicon Valley initiative masterminded by Doug Henton, Kimberley Walesh and John Melville at Collaborative Economics. Although we use civic entrepreneurship in a different context in this report, many of the principles are the same.

We would like to thank the many people in the five case study organisations who gave us their time and ideas so generously while we were doing our research. In addition, we benefited greatly from discussions with: Andrew Foster, at the Audit Commission; Barry Shaw; chief constable of Cleveland; Sylvie Pierce, chief executive of Tower Hamlets; Kingsley Manning at Newchurch Associates; and a group of senior public sector executives on a training course at the Civil Service College, who commented on the main themes before the report was finished.

The Public Management Foundation's input into the report was influenced by discussions among its trustees and in particular the work of Professor Mark Moore from Harvard University.

At Demos, Perri 6's writing on holistic government provided useful background, Tom Bentley made many helpful suggestions and Lindsay Nash edited the text with exemplary competence. The project could not have been completed without Ian Christie's patience and tact.

Charles Leadbeater
April 1998

Preface

Entrepreneurship seems to be a verb! It is not simply a set of actions of a state of being. It is about actively pursuing value.

Entrepreneurship is being celebrated today as never before. It is not only the private sector that seeks ever greater entrepreneurial skills. The voluntary sector too is being energised by new concepts of 'social entrepreneurship'. And the public sector is constantly being urged to become more enterprising in service delivery.

Entrepreneurship is managerial behaviour which consistently exploits opportunities to deliver results beyond one's own capabilities. Entrepreneurship demands vision and a sustained commitment – sometimes in the face of much more mundane things that have to be done. It requires the mustering of new, and often other people's, resources to produce better outcomes.

We know entrepreneurs when we see them. Richard Branson is one, so is Bill Gates, and so was John DeLorean. Some win, others lose. But what is more striking than the risks they take – and more crucial to long-term success – is the sense of enterprise and adventure which they inspire in those around them. Through that, they build up capabilities much bigger than their own and produce results much larger in scope and scale than we should expect.

More important than individual entrepreneurs, however, is entrepreneurship: the pursuit of value. It is that behaviour – simultaneously opportunistic and strategic – from which all managers can learn how to extend their own production. Management is the orchestration of resources to produce value. That is so in both the private sector and the public sector. But because the goals of these sectors are different and because the value to be produced in public enterprise is a social one, it may be that the practice of entrepreneurship in public services offers different lessons and different models, too.

Under New Labour, public managers are being challenged and held to account for producing better outcomes – less ignorance, more employability in those seeking work, safer communities, a healthier nation, among others. This redefinition of the public sector's bottom line calls for new ways of managing that are more value-focused, flexible and opportunistic, that entail cooperation with other agencies and with citizens themselves. All of these are key dimensions of entrepreneurship. All of these depend on outlooks and behaviour which we need to learn more about and which we need to foster.

With the generous support of the National Health Service Executive and Local Government Management Board, the Public Management Foundation and Demos developed a project to explore entrepreneurship in public management and draw out lessons about good practice and how to spread it. The case studies examined here open up a rich seam of learning and development. But as the case studies show, entrepreneurship must be integrated with strategies to meet public demands for fairness, propriety and accountability. These remain fundamental to public service. With the lessons and recommendations from this study, we want to promote civic entrepreneurship, not as a substitute for what good public managers do, but as a new way of thinking and working with which they can help us all produce better social results from the delivery of public services.

Greg Parston
Chair, Public Management Foundation

Introduction

When Norma Redfearn became head teacher at West Walker primary school in Newcastle in 1986 she took over a school in a state of near collapse. About three-quarters of the children were on free school meals. A majority of the parents were unemployed single mothers, who had grown up in workless households. Most of them had hated school as children and had low expectations for their own kids. On any one day about a fifth of the children were not at school. Quite a few of those who did make it to school came late and without having had anything to eat. Only a handful of the West Walker's eighteen class-rooms were occupied. The school seemed to be dying a slow death. Norma Redfearn set out to revive it. In a decade she has transformed it, with the help of the governors, staff and, most of all, the once demoralised parents.

Norma Redfearn realised that to educate her kids she had to educate entire families. To get the parents involved the school had to become more than a set of classrooms: she turned it into a catalyst for community renewal. A decade later the school is transformed. Its attendance record is over 90 per cent and its scores in national tests are improving. Its classrooms are full. But it is much more than that. The school is home to a thriving adult education centre. It has a lively cafe, which provides breakfast for scores of kids each morning. Parents who met while building a nature garden went on to form a housing association that has built an estate of new homes opposite the school. Norma Redfearn understood from the outset that to revive her school she had to be much more than a head teacher; she had to be civic entrepreneur.

Norma Redfearn is an exemplary civic entrepreneur: someone who realises how a public organisation needs to innovate to meet changing demands. She is not alone. All over the public sector, and especially at the frontline, innovators and entrepreneurs are developing new services, often by breaking out of professional and administrative straitjackets. There is a huge amount of creativity and intelligence distributed at the edges of the public sector, where providers meet consumers, teachers meet parents. Take as an example Bob Gregory, a sergeant in the Thames Valley police. Bob Gregory is a long serving officer. He is an imposing figure with a booming voice, the antithesis of trendy, right-on policing, Yet Gregory has pioneered one of the most innovative approaches to youth crime in the country, the Thames Valley restorative justice programme.

From his small office in Aylesbury, Gregory has piloted a new approach to cautioning young first-time offenders. Instead of a traditional caution, usually delivered by an inspector, the Aylesbury scheme asks the young offender to attend a conference, along with the victim of the offence. The offender attends with a parent, grandparent or teacher. The victim also comes with friends or family. The meeting is mediated by Gregory. The aim is to allow the victim to voice their hurt and to get the offender to understand the consequences of their actions. Initially most officers in the Thames Valley force were sceptical. They thought it sounded soft. But it has proved hugely effective. The re-offending rate under the traditional caution is 35 per cent. In the Aylesbury scheme's first year, the re-offending rate was just 4 per cent. Gregory reckons the long term re-offending rate is likely to be about 10 per cent. Gregory explained:

> 'Courts do virtually nothing for victims. They are largely left out of the process. Yet people leave our conferences not feeling like victims anymore. They have been able to confront the offender, voice their feelings and invariably they leave feeling better. For offenders a court appearance is technical, distant; they don't have to engage with it or explain themselves. A caution delivered by an inspector is often something they do not have to engage with. It's like being told off by a headmaster. They grit their teeth and get through it. In our approach they have to look the victim in the eye. Most of them break down. It's much tougher than court.'

Norma Redfearn and Bob Gregory are just two examples of civic entrepreneurs who work in the public sector; there are many others. This book reports some of their stories. The work of people like Norma Redfearn, Bob Gregory and the other civic entrepreneurs profiled in this report will become increasingly important to the public sector, which is still central to most of our lives, despite almost two decades of retrenchment and restructuring. Yet it faces mounting, multiple challenges.

Public sector: trying to keep up with a changing society

The state serves a society which has become increasingly diverse. Different sections of society lead very different lives, do different sorts of work and choose different forms of entertainment. Communities have become increasingly fragmented. People travel considerable distances to work and to shop. Age, gender and race provide vital sources of difference in culture and values. Ours is a society which prizes individuality and difference, and yet the state is far more comfortable with services which are uniform and standardised.

Not only are users of public services more diverse, they are frequently more demanding than they were. Those who can afford high quality public services are increasingly unwilling to accept the poor quality of universally available public services, which have often been starved of investment. There are widening expectations gaps between the public and private services sectors. In the private sector, people are increasingly used to buying services like banking over the telephone or through the Internet. The public sector is under constant pressure to match the pace of service improvement in the private sector.

On top of that, the state has been left to pick up the pieces of an increasingly divided society, in which many millions live in poverty. As a result, the future focus on the public sector is constantly debated. Should public services meet the moderate needs of the majority or focus its limited resources on the far greater needs of the most vulnerable? Should public services aim to provide universal and equivalent standards in schooling, health and housing or should the aim be to fill in the gaps into which the most needy often fall? Managing public organisations in such a demanding and fluid environment is a hugely difficult task.

The public sector has undergone dramatic change in the past two decades. The Conservatives shook up public provision through compulsory competitive tendering, privatisation, restructuring and the introduction of businesslike management methods. Challenged to become more efficient, to produce more 'output' from finite resources, most public sector organisations have responded. Management systems and training programmes have been introduced. Public organisations now go in for strategic business planning, re-engineering, downsizing, unit-cost analysis, performance measurement and quality assurance. Public agencies have earned quality accreditation such as ISO 9000, Investors in People and Chartermarks, and public managers have increasingly acquired MBAs and NVQs.

These changes have undoubtedly brought benefits. In many public agencies customer service has improved, working practices are more flexible and organisations are more open to partnerships. Service costs at the best public sector organisations often compare well with those of private sector competitors. Yet despite these improvements, the public sector still often falls well short of its potential and of public expectations.

In the past few years bodies such as the Audit Commission have started to map that gap between performance and expectation. Its recent report on the youth justice system, Misspent Youth, found that an overwhelming majority of the resources were spent on processing crime after the event. Very little was spent on prevention, rehabilitation or victim support. The youth justice system is processing a social problem but doing far too little to solve it. The reasons for this failure are common to many public institutions: they are focused on outputs rather than outcomes; people and budgets are departmentalised rather than integrated. A worrying number of children emerge from our education system without having gone to lessons or have done exams without having been educated. Too often we judge our commitment to improving health by the amount we spend on hospitals, rather than by the amount that goes on prevention, diet, exercise and primary care. We focus too much on buildings, institutions and their outputs; too little on the outcomes we want and how to best deliver them.

One of the main reasons that the public sector's performance falls short of expectations is that it is slow to learn and change. The most admired private sector companies – Tesco, British Airways, Intel, Hewlett Packard – innovate to create change in products, markets and industries. Traditionally, public sector organisations have done the opposite: they have held on to ways of doing things until they are so clearly obsolete that they are doing harm and, only then, often in the face of a crisis, do they begin the painful process of developing alternatives. The public sector has consistently underestimated the speed of change in society and has been slow to use new technologies. Investment in public sector research and development is pitifully low compared with the private sector. Much of government activity has not changed much from the 1930s and 1950s.

The history of public organisations makes them ill-equipped to learn, as well as to play new roles. Most were designed as large bureaucracies, capable of processing large numbers of cases in identical ways to achieve equity of treatment, with audit trails designed to prevent fraud but not to encourage experimentation and risk taking. They are divided into professionally dominated departments and concentrate activity into narrow specialisms, with little cross-fertilisation of ideas or practices. Public organisations generally have heavy handed management systems, which provide limited autonomy or responsibility to frontline staff. These constraints make it difficult for the public sector to learn, even from itself, and to create more effective services.

Reviving the public sector
We do not need to further restructure or rationalise the public sector but to revive and revitalise it. The Labour government has set itself ambitious social goals in education, employment, crime and health, which it will only achieve if it can galvanize the public sector to new levels of effectiveness. This report is about how to do that, in principle and in practice.

The starting point for renewing the public sector must be a renewal of its relationship with the society it serves. It must proceed from a renewal of purpose. That in turn means focusing the public sector more on the outcomes that society wants, rather than the outputs that public sector organisations produce, to focus on providing better education, community safety, well-being and health, rather than just on examinations, league tables, arrests made, sentences issued and hospital beds occupied. Outputs matter, but only in the context of the wider outcomes that society wants. The pursuit of greater efficiency within the public sector needs to be set within a larger goal of creating a more effective public sector.

It is easier to talk about outcomes than to agree them and measure them. If outcomes are to be achieved they need to be made explicit. Often different outcomes will conflict or matter to different groups within society. Is the outcome we desire from schooling the maximum possible number of children achieving grades A to C in GCSEs, or is it to socialise children, to reduce crime, to support economic regeneration, to educate them for citizenship and a world without stable jobs? Organising and managing the public sector around outcomes is not easy. It can only start, as our case studies show, by the organisation asking fundamental and far-reaching questions about its aims and purpose. Entrepreneurial public organisations constantly ask themselves a range of basic questions. What are we trying to achieve? How do we intend to achieve it? Does our plan to achieve these goals seem plausible to all our partners and users? Do we have the capacity to carry it out? How do we manage the risks inherent in this change?

Asking these questions means shifting the public sector's centre of gravity. It needs to move away from transferring resources from one group to another and towards creating social value and investing in social capital. We need a value creating public sector, which is capable of resolving complex social problems, such as educational underachievement, rather than simply processing it. That shift in emphasis means shifting the terms of the debate about the future of the state away from an obsession about its appropriate size and structure and towards an examination of the capacity and skills it needs to learn and change swiftly.

Of course a renewal of the public sector will require far-reaching organisational change. A focus on outcomes challenges the ways that public agencies have been traditionally organised. Complex social issues such as youth crime, homelessness and educational underachievement do not belong to one department or profession. They can only be addressed by a range of public organisations working together. We need a less bounded public sector, in which organisations and professions become used to collaborating to define problems and implement solutions. The boundaries that bedevil the public sector are not simply those which run between public organisations. As our case studies show, the more entrepreneurial parts of the public sector now recognise that working in partnership with the private sector, community groups and users, is vital not just to bring in more financial resources but to bring in more expertise and imagination. Public sector entrepreneurship is a collaborative process. Effective public sector managers need to excel at collaborative leadership to reconfigure and unlock previously untapped resources.

Britain needs a public sector able to deliver better social outcomes, higher social value and more social capital. Civic entrepreneurship will be an indispensable component of that renewed public service.

Harnessing civic entrepreneurship

The idea of civic entrepreneurship might strike people as odd. Entrepreneurs are generally thought to be bucaneering, egotistical, profit seeking, business people, quite unlike the average public sector manager. Yet there is a growing recognition that the skills of entrepreneurship can be applied in different settings, for non-business goals. In a previous Demos report, The Rise of the Social Entrepreneur, social entrepreneurship was defined in these terms. Social entrepreneurs, often working in deprived communities or in innovative voluntary organisations, are entrepreneurial because they develop imaginative ways to satisfy unmet social needs by using under-utilised resources, such as derelict buildings or people written off by the education system. They are social entrepreneurs rather than business entrepreneurs because their main assets are social, in the form of relationships with supporters, partners and users, and their main goals are social – a better educated, healthier, safer community.

Civic entrepreneurship combines some of the ingredients of social entrepreneurship and entrepreneurship in the business sector. Entrepreneurs in most walks of life are restless, creative, lateral thinking rule breakers. They are frequently storytellers and risk takers, who combine a capacity for visionary thinking with an appetite for opportunism. Many entrepreneurs in the public sector have these characteristics. But civic entrepreneurship takes distinctive skills because public sector organisations are so different from businesses or voluntary bodies. Public organisations are usually larger than most voluntary bodies. They usually have statutory responsibilities and use public money, for which they are held to account. They often have a more formal governance structure, in which managers have to answer to elected members. For these reasons, entrepreneurship in the public sector must be different from entrepreneurship in the business or the voluntary sector.

Three ingredients mark out civic entrepreneurship from other related kinds of entrepreneurship.

First, civic entrepreneurship is necessarily as much about political renewal as it is about managerial change. Public organisations cannot be revitalised unless they renew their sense of purpose: that is a largely political process. Entrepreneurship requires risk taking, to back experimentation and innovation. In the public sector managing those risks requires political skill and leadership. Entrepreneurship in the public sector means bringing together people and resources in new, more effective ways. Often these new collaborations can only be brokered politically. It is not a purely 'managerial' task.

Second, civic entrepreneurship is necessarily collaborative. In the private sector, the entrepreneur is a heroic figure. Entrepreneurship in the public sector is essentially about collaborative leadership, working across boundaries within and beyond organisations.

Third, civic entrepreneurship is about more than individual acts of innovation. Civic entrepreneurs often innovate new products and services, or create the space for others to do that. Yet their role does not end there. A civic innovator might create a new service. A civic entrepreneur is capable of going beyond that to disseminate and embed it, to exploit the maximum social value from it.

Civic entrepreneurs are at work throughout the public sector, at all levels of many different kinds of organisations, large and small, local and national. Coralling this diverse activity into an all-encompassing definition risks over simplifying it. Yet it is worth spelling out the working definition of civic entrepreneurship we employ in this report:

Civic entrepreneurship is the renegotiation of the mandate and sense of purpose of a public organisation, which allows it to find new ways of combining resources and people, both public and private, to deliver better social outcomes, higher social value and more social capital.

We are not suggesting that all public sector managers in all public organisations need to become entrepreneurial overnight. Nor are we proposing that public sector funding and regulation should in future ignore probity in favour of risk taking. We need a much healthier balance in the public sector, so that a far stronger, more widely spread capacity for entrepreneurship goes hand in hand with sound administration and good operational management. Entrepreneurs lose credibility when they neglect the basics of good management.

One of the central propositions of this report is that the best way for the public sector to become more entrepreneurial is to learn from its own best practices in entrepreneurship. There is a great deal more entrepreneurship within the public sector than most people realise. There is a lot of latent entrepreneurship waiting to be untapped by the right kind of management and culture. Growing numbers of local authorities, health authorities, police forces, schools and colleges are experimenting with empowering staff, building new relationships with users and creating partnerships with business. That is the good news. The bad news is that there is still too little entrepreneurship within the public sector, too much of what is attempted is blocked or fails and too little of what is excellent gets taken up by those in the mediocre middle.

If we are to encourage more civic entrepreneurship we need public sector managers at all levels who can: think imaginatively and learn swiftly, understand and assess changing needs, embrace change and take risks, orchestrate different organisations and sets of resources. The skills to do this are not acquired easily. They cannot be transferred through traditional teaching methods. They will not emerge in organisations which punish initiative, direct change in detail from the top or rely on rigid systems for auditing. It will not be enough simply to develop more entrepreneurial managers. They need to be able to deploy those skills in an environment which encourages entrepreneurship. Creating such an environment is the joint task of central government policy makers, auditors and regulators as well as local and national political leaders. Civic entrepreneurship is a collaborative process which is part political, part managerial. It depends upon deploying the right capacities in the right context.

The public sector may benefit from further rationalisation, restructuring and privatisation, but what it most needs is revitalisation. The debate about the state in Britain has been befuddled by crude questions whether the public sector should be larger or smaller. Britain does not need a smaller or larger public sector: it needs a public sector that is much more creative and innovative, inquisitive and intelligent. That means developing an approach to the governance, funding, management and evaluation of the public sector that promotes and spreads civic entrepreneurship. The entrepreneurial organisations profiled in this report show how much scope there is for innovation, how much latent entrepreneurship lies untapped. The lessons they provide should help us to turn ambitions for a more holistic, enabling state into reality.

Each of the case studies that follows has managed to sustain entrepreneurial change over many years. They provide impressive models of public sector entrepreneurship. Yet each local situation is unique. Good practice can never be bottled and applied somewhere else like an ointment. There are no one-size-fits-all, magic solutions to complex social problems. The public sector is highly heterogeneous: entrepreneurial solutions will vary for different organisations, with different histories, cultures, users and political leadership. None of the organisations profiled in this report provide 'the right answer.' Yet each of them has achieved impressive changes and offers some important general lessons about what makes for successful civic entrepreneurship.

West Walker Primary School

West Walker Primary School was almost on its knees when Norma Redfearn arrived as headmistress in June 1986. West Walker is on the outskirts of Newcastle upon Tyne, in an area badly hit by unemployment, poverty and dereliction. The shipyards that once sustained the area are long gone. When Norma Redfearn arrived she found a demoralised community, heavily dependent upon the state and with very low expectations. Many of the parents of children at the school were unemployed, lone mothers. Few had fond memories of their time in education. The school had been designed to take 250 children but due to falling rolls it had just 143 pupils. Only six of its eighteen classrooms were fully-occupied. Had the number of pupils fallen any further the school might have closed. About three-quarters of the pupils were on free school meals. As Norma Redfearn recalls: 'There were no churches, no factories and no work. The school was about the only place for people to come together. If it had closed there would have been nothing.'

Soon after she arrived Norma Redfearn set in train a process which has transformed the school. The educational achievements have been impressive: attendance has improved as have scores in national tests. What is remarkable, however, is the way that Norma Redfearn has brought about the improvement in West Walker's performance. She realised quickly that to educate the children she had to engage the dispirited parents and to do that she had to reinvent the role of the school in its local community. West Walker has become a far better school only because it has been turned it into much more than a traditional school: it has become a focal point for communal renewal which is at the heart of initiatives to improve health, housing, the environment and employment. Norma Redfearn realised that she would only improve the traditional educational outputs of the school, test scores, if she improved educational outcomes: a more inquisitive, better educated community around the school. That is turn meant that parents, and not just the professional teachers, had to have a large hand in defining the role of the school.

Norma Redfearn began by talking to parents over a cup of coffee in the morning. She tried to get them to talk about what they wanted from the school. Their first priority was to do something about the barren windswept playground, which was so unpleasant in winter that many children spent playtimes huddled in doorways. Redfearn contacted architects from the Newcastle Architectural Workshop, who worked intensively with parents and children to turn a plot of muddy ground into an award winning playpark. This was tangible evidence for parents that by working together, with outside allies, they could achieve something.

Staff from the workshop then facilitated an away-day at which staff and parents talked about what they wanted to change about the school. That initial meeting, which allowed staff and parents to think together about the future and agree priorities, was vital to create a consensus and sense of commitment. One priority that emerged immediately was to make better use of the empty classrooms, which left the school vulnerable to vandalism and budget cuts. Redfearn, the parents and the staff drew up a plan to turn the classrooms into a 'community wing', to allow parents to attend classes while their children were at school. The plans were blocked for almost eighteen months by the local authority education department on the grounds that if parents wanted adult education classes they should attend a college of further education. Eventually, with the help of local councillors, one of whom was chairman of the board of governors, the school was allowed to use money from the council leisure department to develop the community wing. This has been a vital development drawing parents into the educational life of the school. Norma Redfearn did not just set out to educate children but entire families who were sceptical of the value of education. The school is more like a family learning centre than a traditional school. The traditional child centred educational activities of the school are enveloped by a wide array of community activities, which have mobilised local support for the school. These wider community activities include:

- A café, used in the mornings and at lunchtime by parents. The cafe runs a breakfast club, attended by 30 to 40 children, funded by the Newcastle Building Society, the North Eastern Co-op, Greggs and Safeway. A free breakfast is served between 8.20am and 8.55am with fresh orange juice, cereal, toast, tea and hot chocolate for any child at the school. Before the breakfast club was created many children arrived at school without having had anything to eat. The club has also improved the school's attendance record. When Redfearn began many children turned up to school at 9.50am. Persistent latecomers now arrive at school on time and those children who were frequently absent are now regular attendees. Norma Redfearn says: 'As educationalists we know that you cannot hope to teach children if they are hungry. To give them a chance of learning you have to make sure they are properly fed.' An application to the district health authority to fund the club was turned down on the grounds that it was not a health initiative.
- The school and playground is open to children out of school hours. About 50 children attend a homework club after school hours.
- The school's community wing comprises a community library for the parents; a computer room used by children and parents; a training room used for classes including assertiveness training, sewing and keep fit; empathy and counselling courses, where parents learn about parenting skills.
- The community wing has become a home for a range of other local authority services, which are becoming more closely integrated with education. The school is host to an Urban Park Warden who looks after the urban park, which runs along the Tyne just below the school. The warden provides nature classes for a number of schools that visit West Walker. The community wing is also home to a social worker who works with lone mothers, many of whom suffered abuse and severe deprivation as children. By siting herself in a school she can be more effective because she is

much closer to the parents, learns about crises more quickly and responds earlier and more effectively to their needs. Parents are more likely to turn to her because she works within an environment they are familiar and comfortable with.

- Two parents were initially trained to provide child care at the West Walker crèche. They went on to set up in business themselves and now employ ten to fifteen local women to provide crèche facilities throughout the area to allow parents to attend training courses.
- The school has helped parents to form lasting relationships, which have helped to improve the environment around the school. The most impressive initiative has been a housing development on the site of the Victorian West Walker primary school. A group of parents who first met through a project to create an environmental garden went on to create a housing association to develop the derelict site. The group, in concert with two larger housing associations, has developed an estate of houses opposite the school, which is home to families with children at the school.

Norma Redfearn and her team of staff, parents and helpers have a range of plans to develop the school's role as an educational resource for the community. They want to create a job club for parents and children to give them both a sense of what jobs are available and what sorts of skills will be needed. This could be the basis for a family work experience programme, in which parents and children from workless households go on work experience projects. A health and fitness room is being created, to highlight the links between fitness, diet, self-esteem and learning.

West Walker's achievements are impressive. Attendance rates have risen from about 80 per cent to more than 95 per cent. The school, which once was two-thirds empty, is now over subscribed. Its scores in national tests have steadily improved. Most significantly, the school has engaged the parents as well as the children in an effort to revive the local community. Norma Readfearn says:

'There is nothing in this that does not come from the parents. Unemployment had created an area in which people were used to other agencies doing things for them: the government, the council, social services. It had bred a passivity that was very undermining. There was a culture of blaming it on other people, waiting for other people to come up with the money or the answers. It wasn't just economically and socially deprived, it was inward looking. The community did not have wide horizons; the poorer it got, the more it turned in on itself. That is what we have to change: not just how children are educated but how the community sees itself.'

Several themes stand out from West Walker's remarkable revival. Norma Redfearn worked closely with parents, staff and governors, to create a common understanding of the outcomes the school was hoping to achieve, rather than setting down narrowly defined professional targets. They started from an holistic assessment of the needs of the families with children at the school. At West Walker education is about health and the environment, diet and housing as well as reading and writing. All of its work has been made possible by working in partnership, with parents and other public agencies, to draw in resources, energy and ideas. Norma Redfearn is an impressive headteacher because she has become a civic entrepreneur.

Thames Valley Police

It was only the second case that sergeant Bob Gregory had handled in Thames Valley's new restorative justice programme. He was still quite sceptical about whether the new approach to cautioning young offenders would work. On the face of it the case seemed simple enough. A young boy had been caught stealing a near neighbour's car. An unremarkable, quickly resolved, commonplace vehicle theft. Under the traditional system for cautioning first-time offenders, the youth would have been given a stern lecture by an inspector. He would not have been required to show much understanding of the consequences of his actions, nor to offer any reparation to the victim, who would have learned the outcome of the case with a standard letter. The restorative justice programme, which had then just started in Aylesbury, takes a different, much more demanding approach. The offender was asked to attend a meeting accompanied by his mother and organised by Gregory, at which the victim and his family would explain what had happened to them. The meeting is known as a restorative conference.

The victim of the crime, a middle age man, had rushed home from work to get changed and catch a train to London to see a friend who was in hospital. He was changing upstairs when through his bedroom window he saw the young boy steal his car. He ran out of the house after the car. After a few minutes he returned panting to get in a neighbour's car to give chase. His wife was deeply alarmed. Only three months before the incident her husband had by-pass surgery following an heart attack. His wife was convinced that the stress of the chase would give him another heart attack. She thought it was the last that she might see of her husband. In panic she ran to get her son who was playing football in a nearby park. As she ran towards her son, gesticulating, she collapsed unconscious and had to be rushed to hospital herself. The theft of the car had left the family distraught.

When the family started to tell its story during the restorative conference the boy hardly seemed to take note. He stared out of the window and then at his shoes. He seemed disrespectful. He fiddled with a pen. The atmosphere in the room grew tense. But as the victim's wife started to explain how worried she had become that she might never see her husband alive again, the boy started to look at her. Finally he started concentrating, looking her square in the eye. When the wife finished her tale, the young offender collapsed, his head resting on the table. He sobbed uncontrollably for ten minutes.

When the boy had recovered, he began to apologise profusely, not just to the family but to his mother. The victims' son talked honestly about his own scrapes with the law when he was young. The two families travelled home together. They remain on friendly terms.

That story, in a nutshell, is the case for restorative justice. The restorative caution is a significant innovation in what is one of the police force's most basic 'products'. It involves a completely different philosophy and practice of policing. This is how a leaflet published by the Thames Valley force describes the change in approach:

'Most western criminal justice systems focus primarily on the need to process and punish offenders. Victims, and others affected, often perceive themselves as mere bystanders. Offenders do no appear to be always called to account for their actions. Restorative justice offers a balanced approach to meeting the needs of victims, communities and offenders.

'Those who have been affected talk about the impact of crime, instead of the professionals of the criminal justice system talking for them. A restorative conference is one way of allowing all those who have been affected to meet in a safe environment and [it] has a key role within restorative justice. A trained person who invites those present to talk about what has happened facilitates it. Usually there is an opportunity at the end of the conference to come to an agreement about reparation. This helps victims to feel restored after the crime.

'Traditionally offenders are never required to explain their actions or to listen to details of the personal harm they have caused. In a courtroom their sense of accountability is further diminished by the depersonalised, technical nature of the proceedings and by the mitigation process, in which their lawyer tries to shed as much responsibility as possible for the crime. By contrast, restorative conferencing means that they are confronted with what they have done, learn about the conse-quences for other people and take responsibility for their actions.'

Restorative justice is a more efficient and more effective way of issuing a first-time caution. Victims feel empowered and restored by it. They leave the conference no longer feeling like victims. Offenders have to make an effort to understand the consequences of their actions. Restorative justice does not impose a sense of shame from the outside; it works on the offender's own sense of self-esteem. This year, Thames Valley police will issue most of its first-time cautions for young people using restorative justice. The story of how it developed this new approach and spread it across a large police force contains lessons for all public sector organisations.

The new Thames Valley approach to cautioning had a long, complex gestation. It was fed from several sources. One important source was a youth crime initiative developed in Milton Keynes in the early 1990s. Under the leadership of Caroline Nicholl, then area commander in Milton Keynes, the local force developed a new philosophy of policing. Nicholl's sometimes controversial philosophy was that the police's job was not so much law enforcement, as helping to create a safer, self-policing society. That meant policing through partnerships with retail-ers, schools and the social services. Milton Keynes is a new town, and in the 1980s there was a recognition among the police and social services that a relatively young, expanding mobile population would present particular issues of public safety and law and order. People below the age of twenty make up about 33 per cent of Milton Keynes' population, compared with about 28 per cent of the population of as a whole. This age group is responsible for a disproportionate amount of detected crime, particularly burglaries and vehicle theft.

At Caroline Nicholl's prompting a Youth Crime Strategy Group, bringing together the police, probation services, education, housing and social services, started to share more information about their resources and working methods. The aim was to establish a better joint understanding of the shared problems that the agencies dealing with young offenders faced. The aim was to encourage the agencies to come to a joint view of the outcomes they wanted, a lower rate of youth crime, rather than the specific outputs they were responsible for, such as cases processed. A seminar of operational staff worked through detailed case studies of the lifecycle of young offenders, tracing how each agency dealt with the person in the course of his youth. The seminar's conclusions were :

- there was no overall strategy for the different agencies to work within
- agencies thought about their problems and their resources in departmentalised ways, which tended to exaggerate the scale of the problem and minimise the available resources
- information sharing was limited: social services shared little information with schools who rarely talked to the police
- there was very little effort at diverting people from crime; most of the effort went into processing crime after it had occurred.

Following that seminar in 1993, the Youth Crime Strategy Group carried out an audit of the criminal justice system in Milton Keynes, funded by Marks & Spencer, in an effort to establish how money was spent, on what, by whom. That audit found that £16m a year was spent on criminal justice in Milton Keynes but less than 1 per cent was spent on victims; much more was spent on reacting to crime rather than preventing it, there was very little contact with offenders and it was usually too little, too late. That audit helped to establish the financial case for more effective, earlier intervention to reduce youth crime. By highlighting the inefficiencies of the current approach it made it more legitimate and less risky to develop an alternative.

A subsequent television documentary, which analysed a young burglar's career between the ages of twelve and 25, found that the cost to the criminal justice system over thirteen years of repeat offending might be as high as £2.5 million. It found that such a young offender would probably have first come to the notice of social services at the age of four because of his family background and teachers at the age of seven or eight, due to learning difficulties or disruptive behaviour. Yet the agencies that dealt with the young offender early on rarely talked to those which dealt with him later in life. That analysis highlighted the pay-off from coordinated, early intervention to prevent social problems at the age of four leading to criminal behaviour later in life. The media exposure helped to create a sense of public expectation and scrutiny on the agencies involved to cooperate.

All the agencies involved recognised that they would benefit from a more integrated, cooperative approach. Yet there was still a significant problem: funding. Public sector budgets are departmental; yet the problems the public sector addresses cut across those departments. There was no budget for an inter-departmental approach to youth crime. The solution came after Thames Valley applied for a £600,000 grant from the Home Office Programme Development Unit, which, with a further contribution of £150,000 from the Thames Valley force, provided funding for a three year programme to develop an integrated, preventive approach to youth crime. As a result, the Milton Keynes force is implementing a youth crime prevention strategy on three levels.

At the primary level there will be greater emphasis on educating young people about the consequences of crime, especially for victims. At a secondary level, a fund has been set aside for a ten strong, multidisciplinary team to work on an intensive twelve week programme with disaffected young people excluded from school. The aim is to create a range of alternatives to school exclusion, given that children excluded from school are highly likely to drift into crime. The third level has been to develop an alternative approach to cautioning, focused on mediation and reparation rather than punishment and process. This has been most used in the innovative Milton Keynes retail theft initiative, which the police force has developed by working closely with retailers.

The Milton Keynes youth crime strategy involved painstaking work to establish the case for a different approach to law enforcement, based on a radically different philosophy of policing and punishment. It focused on outcomes rather than outputs, prevention rather than reaction, working in partnership rather than within the confines of professional disciplines. The restorative justice programme, which is not confined to youth crime and is now spreading across the force, builds on many of the principles of the holistic approach developing in Milton Keynes. Thames Valley's Chief Constable, Charles Pollard, had come across restorative justice in Australia, where police officers had learned from Maori justice in New Zealand, which stressed the roles of mediation, reconciliation and reparation rather than punishment and due process.

Bob Gregory was asked to pilot the restorative justice scheme in the Aylesbury area in April 1995. Initially it was not successful, in part because offenders were given the choice of opting into the scheme and few chose to do so. Gregory admits that he was unprepared for the change in outlook and behaviour that restorative conferencing would require from him. From January 1996 the restorative conference became an opt-out scheme: offenders would normally be cautioned this way, unless they opted not to.

Evidence of the success of the scheme is still tentative. The recidivism rate (the rate of re-offending) among young offenders cautioned in the traditional way is about 35 per cent. The recidivism rate among young offenders cautioned through the restorative conference was just 4 per cent in the first year. Gregory reckons the long-term recidivism rate will be 10 per cent. The traditional caution, accompanied by a great deal of paper work, took five and a half hours to complete. The restorative conference can take as little as an hour to conduct, although it often takes much longer to prepare the victims for it. Almost all of that time is invested in the victim and the offender, rather than in paperwork. Gregory maintains that the scheme should not be judged by those statistics.

The main value of the restorative justice programme is intangible: it helps the victims of crime to stop feeling victimised. This is born out by more substantial research to monitor the effectiveness of the Australian programme. A study by the Australian National University of the experience of restorative justice in Canberra found that 79 per cent of offenders felt ashamed of their actions, compared with 66 per cent who went through the courts; 47 per cent said it increased their respect for the police, compared with 18 per cent who went through the courts. The effects on victims were even more pronounced. About 83 per cent were awarded restitution and 74 per cent received an apology through the restorative justice programme, compared with only 8 per cent and 14 per cent respectively through the courts system. Only 6 per cent of victims who attended a restorative conference left fearing re-victimisation, compared with almost a fifth of those who went through the courts.

Pollard and other senior officers believed the new approach was an innovative piece of best practice that should be spread throughout the force but it was far from clear how that should be done. The new caution requires officers to listen and prompt more than they talk and lecture. That meant introducing a training programme that would challenge deeply held tacit assumptions about how the police should go about their job. Spreading best practice would take patience, persuasion and flexibility and a significant change in culture.

Pollard had set up the Crime Partnership Consultancy, a small unit at headquarters with the task of identifying good ideas and spreading them through the organisation. A couple of officers within the consultancy, Sergeant Andy Bird and Inspector Ewart Watson, developed a strategy for implementing the Aylesbury pilot force-wide, which they put to Pollard. They recommended a flexible approach so that each of the fourteen areas within the force could be given time to implement restorative justice at their own speed and in their own way, to maximise local control and responsibility. The areas within the force were given a target of having a restorative caution in place by April 1998.

There was no single civic entrepreneur at Thames Valley. The restorative justice innovation has succeeded, thus far, because entrepreneurship emerged at all levels of the police service. Civic entrepreneurship is rarely, if ever, an heroic, individualistic activity. It is almost always a collaborative venture. In Thames Valley different people were entrepreneurial at different stages of the process. Caroline Nicholl was a civic entrepreneur as an area commander. She had an inspirational vision of a different kind of criminal justice system. But her vision would have been nothing without the work of other people to translate it into practice. Bob Gregory is a civic entrepreneur. He took risks with his career and reputation to pilot the controversial approach. Bob Gregory turned an idea into a piece of good practice. Andy Bird and Ewart Watson, a sergeant and an inspector, have been organisational entrepreneurs. They spotted the potential of the Aylesbury pilot and devised a way to spread it force-wide and thereby maximise its social value. Andy Bird and Ewart Watson were not inventors; their contribution was to devise a way to exploit an invention.

Finally, the context in which all these people worked was in part created by Charles Pollard, himself, who understood the need to create spaces in which innovation, experimentation and new thinking could take place and to match that with a commitment to realistic implementation. If an organisation is to become entrepreneurial, it needs entrepreneurial action at all levels and at different stages of developing a new service.

Kirklees Metropolitan Authority

The public sector has too little space for innovation and entrepreneurship. Private sector companies have research and development budgets and new product development teams. Venture capitalists are one source of capital for entrepreneurs who want to turn bright ideas into businesses. Government policy has long recognised the value of small enterprise in creating new businesses and jobs. Yet the public sector lacks any effective equivalent for developing new ideas and turning them into new products and services. Innovation has to be conducted within organisations, on the job and frequently on the run as well. Kirklees Metropolitan Authority in Yorkshire stands out as a case study of how an organisation can restructure to create more space for entrepreneurship.

The restructuring at Kirklees was led by two men who in their own right stand as civic entrepreneurs. Robert Hughes, the recently retired chief executive, was the managerial architect of many of the changes. A former pop star, Hughes is a dynamic, iconoclastic, outspoken and inspirational leader who is impatient for change and sets ambitious targets. It was his frustration with the traditional departmental bureaucracy at the authority that spurred many of the subsequent changes. However, Hughes could not have succeeded without the support of the council's leader, Sir John Harman, who played a critical role in creating the political space for entrepreneurship and risk taking. Harman's leadership helped to sweep away many of the traditional politics of committees and public meetings. It was this alliance between a reforming political leadership and a modernising management team that created the space for entrepreneurship to flourish.

The reorganisation at Kirklees has created at least three 'spaces' in which innovation and entrepreneurship can emerge. First, by focusing the senior management and political leaders on the strategic issues facing the authority, such as community safety and the environment, the council has been able to renew its sense of purpose by concentrating on the outcomes, rather than the outputs, it should deliver. Second, by devolving operational responsibility to line managers it has created more space for innovation and experimentation with service delivery. Third, by stressing the importance of partnerships with outsiders, such as the churches, community groups and private companies, the authority has encouraged its officers to explore new more creative relationships as the way to develop services. These partnerships have not only brought the council access to new resources but also new ideas and expertise.

Entrepreneurship in strategy

Robert Hughes introduced radical changes to the structure of management at Kirklees that were designed to create the space for an integrated senior management team to focus on strategic issues facing the authority, rather than operational minutiae or departmental baronies and budgets. The small senior management team's job is to identify and articulate the outcomes the authority should be trying to achieve for its community. Hughes explained: 'The authority has to take its lead from what society wants, not what we can deliver. Our goals need to come from social aspirations not council departments.' That means focusing the senior executives on external demands and future trends. Hughes hopes that by giving the senior managers this strategic task and no operational budgets to manage, the authority will have created a capacity for organisational renewal. 'The idea is that we should not just do better what we already do, but find those things we should be doing which we aren't.' he says.

A small, executive team of about five people, working closely with council leaders, is charged with addressing strategic issues, such as environmental policies, community safety and youth work. Politicians and senior managers meet each week on a policy board, which is the heart of strategic policy making in the council. Ideas can be put to the policy board from anywhere in the organisation. Once the policy board

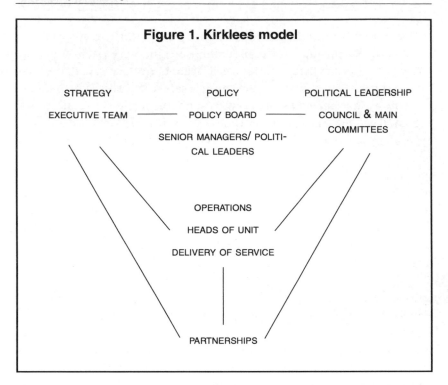

Figure 1. Kirklees model

has agreed a strategy, for instance to improve the council's environmental recycling, a senior executive is tasked to pull together the various operational departments which will have a role in delivering it. Executives are judged on their performance according to the tasks they are given, rather than the size of the budget or department they control. However, change has not been painless. Several senior departmental managers were sacked to make way for the new structure and layers of middle management have been thinned out.

Operational entrepreneurship

By focusing senior managers on strategic issues, operational line management has been given more space to innovate in the way that they deliver services, in theory at least. Departmental managers are expected to collaborate more than in other authorities. Cross-functional team working is increasingly commonplace in Kirklees. One example of how a relatively junior middle manager exploited this space is the creation of the Kirklees talk-back panel.

The authority has developed new ways of staying abreast of user views through an initiative taken by the research department. The authority had used public opinion surveys in 1991 and 1993 to gauge local views about the council. However, repeated requests to the market research department for more regular and more specific market research persuaded officials in the research department that it needed a more regular and flexible device to test public opinion. Deborah Wilkinson, the junior manager who came up with the idea for the talk-back panel explained:

'It is quite easy for managers of particular services to test the views of particular client groups who use their services. It is far more difficult to organise regular and timely surveys of opinion across the entire authority.'

Wilkinson led the initiative to create a new way of testing public opinion, by working in tandem with the health authority, itself an innovative partnership at the time. They recruited a panel of 1,000 electors, by sending letters to 10,000 electors asking them to volunteer to answer three postal surveys a year. The panel generally provides an 80 per cent response rate. The panel is a ready-made device for testing public opinion on planned initiatives such as pricing for services, plans to improve information about local markets and proposed names for one-stop shops.

An example of how the division of labour between strategic and operational management can work is the development of Kirklees frontline service delivery. The executive team and the policy board decided to make improved frontline service delivery a priority across the authority's services by rationalising the authorities 119 separate frontline service points into nine one-stop shops; creating a more integrated telephone answering system, involving possibly a call centre, to handle the 70 per cent of contacts with the council which are made by telephone; improving electronic access to the council, through a trial of public access points to a Web site and video conferencing kiosks.

The aims and principles of the strategy were set out from the centre: to create a more seamless, accessible service for users in which a high proportion of inquiries are dealt with at the point of contact rather than through referral to a specialist department. Yet the delivery of the changes is a responsibility of line management. Each aspect of the improvement plan is the responsibility of an operational head of service, with that cross-functional team of operational managers reporting to a member of the executive board.

Entrepreneurship through partnership

A third aspect of entrepreneurship at Kirklees is innovation through partnerships. Ken Gillespie has one of those arcane, unilluminating titles that seem to abound in the public sector. He is manager of the 'Rolling Programme'. Gillespie manages Kirklees' burgeoning network of relationships with private, voluntary and community partners. The most obvious, and in some ways the most impressive, of these is the partnership which created the state-of-the-art McAlpine Sports stadium close to centre of Huddersfield. The stadium, which has a worldwide reputation, is a modern monument to civic entrepreneurship. The private sector could not have built it on its own. The local football and rugby clubs did not have the resources, nor did the public sector. Instead Kirklees brokered a highly creative public-private partnership which has built a stadium that is neither purely public nor purely private: it is a community asset.

Kirklees' first significant partnership was a 1989 joint venture with the Henry Boot building company to redevelop council property for housing, retail and industrial uses. The partnership's largest project is the redevelopment of part of Huddersfield town centre. The partnership gives the council a share of profits from development. But just as importantly the long-term relationship has brought Kirklees access to expertise which has allowed it to address development issues it would have found difficult to tackle on its own. The Kirklees Henry Boot Partnership paved the way for the council to form the partnership to develop the McAlpine Stadium, providing a new home for Huddersfield's football and rugby clubs.

The spur for the stadium partnership came from national policy: the Taylor Report on Sports Ground Safety. Neither the football nor the rugby club could afford to rebuild their existing facilities or to build a new stadium, to meet the standards laid down in the Taylor Report.

The clubs faced long-term decline from falling gate takings. Kirklees council recognised the importance of the clubs to the town's morale and its economy. It also recognised an opportunity to develop a tract of derelict land close to the town centre. Through the Kirklees Henry Boot Partnership the council devised a way to redevelop the old Huddersfield Town Football Club into a retail park. The funds from that development provided the financial foundations for the award winning stadium.

Most of the main decisions about the project were taken quickly between the council leaders, its senior executives, the senior executives of the clubs and the private sector partners. Between them. the partners raised pledges of £8 million to create a joint company, Kirklees Stadium Development Limited, owned 40 per cent by the council, 40 per cent by the football club and 20 per cent by the rugby club. The joint company was to design, construct and manage the multi-use stadium for the partners. The council provided financial guarantees as well as funds from the sale of land.

The elegant, futuristic stadium opened with three stands in August 1994. It is far more than a sports facility. The council is determined it should play a wider role in community regeneration. It regards the stadium as an investment in the town's social capital. As well as a wide range of football and rugby games, including international fixtures, the stadium has hosted rock and classical concerts, shows and exhibitions. A fourth 4,000-seater stand will include a multi-purpose leisure complex, with a swimming pool, health club, restaurant, and conference centre. Council officials believe this leisure partnership could show how to redevelop its other leisure facilities through public-private partnerships. Many of the jobs building and running the stadium have been filled by staff from the Stadium Employment Partnership, which has gone on to play a wider role in local economic regeneration.

The partnership has been a way for the council to multiply the resources applied to the project and so deliver a much better social outcome than if either the public or the private sector had taken on the scheme on its own. The council has been able to use its financial stake as a catalyst for private sector investment. The replacement cost of building a new sports stadium was about £30 million. The related leisure and retail investments have been worth about £50 million. The development has created perhaps 1,000 jobs. About 500,000 people a year visit the complex. Yet the council has only invested 'usable' capital of about £3.8 million in the project in return for a 40 per cent stake in the company which runs the stadium. This is an outstanding example of the local state acting as a catalyst for public, private and communal renewal.

The stadium's success, combined with the opportunities created by the Private Finance Initiative has spurred the council to develop its partnership programme. The Kirklees–Churches Partnership Trust has been formed to fund community projects. Another partnership is funding housing development. The council is examining the role that a public-private partnership might play in facilities management of public buildings, such as security, catering and cleaning of schools and other buildings.

Learning from failure

Kirklees is a highly innovative local authority. To innovate you have to take risks – there are bound to be failures. Managing failure is a vital part of entrepreneurship, because failure often provides better lessons than success. Kirklees' approach to learning from failure stands out in its approach of household recycling.

The idea that more household waste should be recycled looked good on paper and seemed to command wide public support. Opinion surveys showed a huge majority of electors supported the idea. Yet implementing an effective recycling scheme proved far more difficult in practice, even though the initiative appeared well planned. In 1993, the council launched a pilot scheme of two types of rubbish collection rounds for 12,000 households to promote recycling. The six month trial seemed to be a success and so the council decided to extend the scheme over the entire authority, over five years, with five rounds of 6,000 households moving onto recycling each year. The eventual savings from smaller rubbish collection crews and fewer black bin bags would pay for the up-front investment in the bins. Over the first two years, progress appeared to be good but thereafter the scheme quickly ran into problems.

It emerged that the quality of the recyclable materials was highly variable, especially when collection routines were disrupted over holiday periods. The council did not have enough information about what kind of rubbish its households generated. Managers had based their projections on the waste generated by a notional average household. But it transpired that households with large extended families generated more rubbish and less recyclable rubbish than expected. In shared student households, frequently no one took responsibility for the rubbish. In large Asian households, women looked after the rubbish, but official council communications, even when translated into several languages, rarely reached them. Also, the communication programme linked with the change was far too complex. There was too little full-time support: just one full-time officer was responsible for the environmental education of the 30,000 people a year expected to switch to the scheme. Partnerships with the waste management companies handling the recycled material were not strong enough. Rubbish collection staff had been poorly prepared. The crews had no incentive to send back a bin with contaminated waste because that simply meant they would have more work to do later.

In the past year, the council has taken a stronger line on enforcement: an official travels with every crew to check on the quality of the recyclable material. If a household persistently puts contaminated waste in its recycling bin the council warns that it might have its bins taken away. About 1,600 warning letters have been sent out so far and 300 bins have been removed. Improved education and tougher enforcement has dramatically improved the quality of the recyclable waste. Yet the council's performance is still well short of its target. The authority set out to recycle 25 per cent of household waste. Five years after the scheme was first launched it is only recycling 3 per cent. The current approach to recycling will not get the authority anywhere near its goal. The lessons from failure are as instructive as Kirklees' successes. Politicians and policy makers at the top led the initiative without thinking through carefully enough how it would be implemented. There were no entrepreneurs lower down the organisation to take it up. Users were not involved in designing the scheme in detail. Although the general idea of recycling was popular, the council had done too little to win support for its particular approach.

Dorset Health Authority

Barry Robinson is a general practitioner who came to the conclusion that to be a better doctor he had to become a civic entrepreneur. Dr Robinson came into the profession late in life, after a career as an engineer. The professional demarcation lines that doctors erect around them do not impress him. His clinic in Lyme Regis is one model for a more integrated, holistic, primary healthcare service. Dr Robinson runs the whole of the health-care budget, including emergency services, for about 8,000 patients and two GP practices in Dorset. By handling all the resources and striking a deal with social services, the unit has broken down traditional barriers which separate different arms of the caring services. Dr Robinson's clinic has some of the characteristics of a fundholding GPs practice. A patient can enter his clinic and access a wide range of health services, such as specialist cancer treatments. What is novel about Dr Robinson's clinic is the other preventive, community services it provides in addition. Patients can get a meals-on-wheels service or counselling from social workers who deal with child abuse. The unit employs, among others, a social worker, health visitors, psychiatric and other specialist nurses, physiotherapists, a chiropodist and a counsellor.

The unit has helped to transform local services. Cataract operations, for example, – 100 a year – are now treatable as day cases in the local community hospital because services for patients coming out of hospital are so much better managed. There is a hospital-at-home scheme, as well as terminal care programme. Dr Robinson argues that by having one overall budget it is easier to shift around resources to meet changing demand. Traditional barriers between doctors and nurses are easier to break down. Cost savings generated through efficiency gains can go to fund improvements elsewhere within the unit. The unit operates as a non-profit making limited company and the doctors are employed as family doctors.

This innovative, integrated approach to primary healthcare has won a lot of plaudits and helped to inform Dorset Health Authority's developing approach to planning primary care. The practice is not without its problems. Dr Robinson has run into the politics of his profession. In 1997, he entered a partnership dispute with other doctors over the unit's management and priorities. Yet, despite these difficulties, Dr Robinson's practice has helped inform Dorset Health Authority's innovative and developing approach to a more integrated healthcare system.

The authority has played a vital role in innovation by finding new ways to recombine the resources of the health service more effectively. It has done this in large part by using its own resources to leverage other resources controlled by hospital and general practitioners. It has also opened up the space for a more entrepreneurial approach to healthcare by fostering creative collaboration between clinicians, users, managers and outside partners. The authority's work is a case study of how an intermediate body, which stands between Whitehall and local service delivery, can help to promote civic entrepreneurship.

Edward Colgan, director of strategy explained how the authority had gone about building its credibility: 'Innovations of this kind will only work if the authority is seen by doctors to have credibility based on its ability to deliver on the basics of waiting lists and financial management. If you do not deliver on the basics you will not win the credibility you need to go forward with more innovative schemes. The only power you have with independent contractors is influence, peer pressure and incentives. Imposing change will not work.'

In 1992–93 the authority persuaded general practitioners to become involved in a planning process, to encourage them to think more strategically about how to meet the health needs of the local population rather than concentrating solely on delivering their basic medical services contract. This involved asking GPs to examine how they cooperated with non-GP services such as physiotherapy, psychiatric care and community health councils. The authority had no statutory powers to require GPs to take part in such an exercise. Its only lever was to use peer pressure among professionals to help to spread best practice. It also helped to create GP networks, around twelve local purchasing alliances.

The authority plans to build on its involvement with GPs by creating personalised, integrated care plans for six major illnesses, such as heart and renal disease, cancer, diabetes, asthma and mental illnesses. These personalised plans would cut across the boundaries of the system, which divides care into primary and secondary, community and specialist. These divisions make it very difficult to organise a seamless, integrated programme for patients. Often problems slip between the cracks in the system. Instead of a patient being passed between the separate parts of the system, a personalised care plan should allow for more seamless treatment with better communication between the primary, secondary and community arms of the health service. The authority has acted as a broker to convene interdisciplinary working groups to map the optimal pathways for care and to make sure patients are better informed about the choices facing them. Personalised care plans can only be developed if all the agencies involved are brought together to address the needs of a patient, through a single decision making body. The authority's role as a broker/convenor is to facilitate such collaborative problem solving.

The authority has provided £395,000 for the development of the new approach, an investment in innovation. The project teams are being led by practitioners, clinicians and managers with relevant expertise from hospitals and clinics within the authority. However, to lever in more resources the authority has taken the novel step of involving private sector partners at a very early stage. Five pharmaceuticals companies have expressed an interest in being involved with the local projects in the following areas: Glaxo-Wellcome (asthma and diabetes); Lilly Industries (severe mental illness); Smith Kline Beecham (heart disease); Norvatis (renal disease); and Zeneca (cancers). The implementation plan for the personalised care plans, written in June 1997, said: 'The authority will be looking wherever possible for support from the pharmaceutical companies to be in the form of staffing to assist in local development and implementation work.' The authority has thus created the basis for a novel private-public partnership in health service innovation, using its own resources to lever in resources from the private sector.

As importantly, the authority has set out to win legitimacy for a new approach by explicitly involving patients and their families in the redesign of services. The implementation plan says:

'The project groups will at an early stage need to identify user representatives who will need to be pro-actively involved in the work of the project group. A key measure of the success of each project will be how effectively patients have been engaged in developing personalised care management.'

The implementation plan also sets out a role for organisational innovators to work collaboratively on the organisational implications of delivering the optimal care pathways devised by the groups. Equally striking is the role to be played by an independent evaluation and dissemination unit based at the Health Services Management Unit at the University of Manchester. The unit's role is to learn lessons and spread best practice. It's task is to 'report on the significance of Dorset's work for the NHS as a whole and identify work elsewhere in the UK and internationally which may in turn inform the Dorset programme.'

Entrepreneurship in the public sector cannot be an heroic, individualistic activity. It necessarily involves negotiating change and patiently building more collaborative approaches. That is why the work of the Dorset Health Authority counts as civic entrepreneurship. It has patiently won a mandate from practitioners and users to develop a different approach to six major diseases and found ways to bring to bear new resources, through public private partnerships, to invest in that innovation.

South Somerset District Council

Mel Usher is chief executive of South Somerset District Council, which has a budget of about £70 million a year to serve more than 140,000 people. He gives every impression of not knowing what is going on most of the time. Usher revels in his ignorance. He puts it this way:

> 'Ignorance is the only option. You have to let power slip away. One person could only know everything that was going on by slowing things down and simplifying things. It might make you feel more powerful, in charge, but it would be a disaster. You have to let power go, that is the only way to become more efficient and more creative while spending less money. My job as chief executive is to help shape a broad sense of direction, to help to set priorities and to bring people together to help them come up with better solutions.'

Usher and his colleagues at South Somerset have overseen one of the most radical reorganisations ever attempted within a local authority. It has involved dismantling a traditional, hierarchical management structure, replete with seven departments, chief and deputy officers, and replacing it with four local areas, each of which is given wide latitude to decide how best to deliver council services. The four areas are brought together by a small central executive team, which plays the role of convenor and catalyst. South Somerset exemplifies the essentially collaborative nature of entrepreneurship in the public sector. Its renewal has been fed by initiatives taken by politicians, senior managers and frontline staff. Its decentralisation programme has succeeded, only after a false start, because it has released resources that were previously trapped within departmental hierarchies. The key to South Somerset's success is not so much is reformed structure but the culture it has created among the staff and politicians. What is striking about South Somerset is that everyone sings from the same song sheet, from the chief executive and the leader of the council to the receptionist at the rubbish dump. They all talk about the value of self-management, entrepreneurship, initiative, learning, collaboration and judging performance by outcomes.

South Somerset has transformed itself through two waves of reorganisation. After the Liberal Democrats won control of the council from the Conservatives in 1987 the new ruling group tried to implement many of the ideas on decentralisation that they had developed in opposition. However it was not until late 1991 when the council appointed Mel Usher as chief executive, that the changes gathered momentum. In November 1991 a traditional, hierarchical local authority committee and management structure was swept away. The council was divided into four areas, each of which was run by a committee of members who were responsible for the provision of all council services in their areas. This first stab at decentralisation was at best a qualified success. The areas really only had control over housing decisions. Many other services, such as environmental health, were still under central political and management control. Three central committees still controlled most resources. The council had decentralised delivery but not decision making.

Several factors led the council to go for a much more radical upheaval in 1995. Many members felt deeply frustrated that more power was not in local hands and that they could not have more of an impact on policies affecting their wards. As council leader Sue Millar put it; 'Many of our members had been community activists. They did not want to waste all their time on committees.' Frontline staff were also dissatisfied. They had been ill-prepared for working outside a traditional hierarchy. As a result many felt unable to exploit the freedom that decentralisation was intended to give them. National policy was another spur. The Banham review of unitary authorities provoked the council to rethink from scratch how it wanted to organise itself. In this second wave of changes, which also involved the sale of the old council head offices, a swathe of senior officers were either made redundant or transferred to jobs in the areas. A high proportion of staff were invited to change jobs, moving them out of central hierarchical departments to work in teams delivering services in the four areas. (The organisation of the council is set out in Figure 2; Figure 3 shows the council's organisation prior to restructuring.)

South Somerset's reorganisation has created room for entrepreneurship in two ways. First, it freed resources by disbanding much of the traditional departmental hierarchies and committees which absorbed so much of the time of council officers and elected members. Senior executives believed that too much of the resources of these hierarchical departments were tied up simply servicing the power structure, rather than delivering value to citizens and consumers. The reorganisation freed up resources by eliminating much of the superstructure of senior management in these departments. Yet on its own that would not have been enough to promote more entrepreneurship. The second step was to make sure these resources flowed into new ways of working and new staff roles for staff which the reorganisation created. The restructuring had an impact on virtually every job in the council and for many of those jobs the scope for initiative and entrepreneurship was increased.

Senior managers acquired a clearer responsibility for focusing the council on the outcomes it wanted to achieve, rather than managing outputs. The head office of the council is regarded not as the top of the organisation, but as the centre, servicing the areas and making it possible for frontline staff to do a better job.

This more strategic role for the centre implied that senior managers could not and would not attempt to manage the details of provision. This was left up to each area to decide. To exploit this decentralisation, however, the council had to inculcate a culture of self-management and local initiative. This involved frontline staff, particularly the new community advisers, taking on far more responsibility for initiating new services, for instance in conjunction with the voluntary sector. Initially, in the 1991 reorganisation, the frontline staff were not ready to exploit their new freedom. It was only after further training and preparation that this happened following the second wave of decentralisation in 1995.

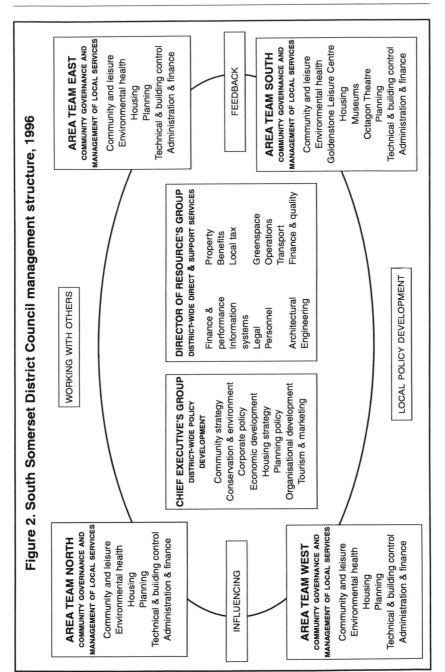

Figure 2. South Somerset District Council management structure, 1996

WORKING WITH OTHERS

AREA TEAM EAST
COMMUNITY GOVERNANCE AND MANAGEMENT OF LOCAL SERVICES

Community and leisure
Environmental health
Housing
Planning
Technical & building control
Administration & finance

FEEDBACK

AREA TEAM SOUTH
COMMUNITY GOVERNANCE AND MANAGEMENT OF LOCAL SERVICES

Community and leisure
Environmental health
Goldenstone Leisure Centre
Housing
Museums
Octagon Theatre
Planning
Technical & building control
Administration & finance

DIRECTOR OF RESOURCE'S GROUP
DISTRICT-WIDE DIRECT & SUPPORT SERVICES

Finance & performance
Information systems
Legal
Personnel
Architectural
Engineering

Property
Benefits
Local tax

Greenspace
Operations
Transport
Finance & quality

CHIEF EXECUTIVE'S GROUP
DISTRICT-WIDE POLICY DEVELOPMENT

Community strategy
Conservation & environment
Corporate policy
Economic development
Housing strategy
Planning policy
Organisational development
Tourism & marketing

LOCAL POLICY DEVELOPMENT

AREA TEAM NORTH
COMMUNITY GOVERNANCE AND MANAGEMENT OF LOCAL SERVICES

Community and leisure
Environmental health
Housing
Planning
Technical & building control
Administration & finance

INFLUENCING

AREA TEAM WEST
COMMUNITY GOVERNANCE AND MANAGEMENT OF LOCAL SERVICES

Community and leisure
Environmental health
Housing
Planning
Technical & building control
Administration & finance

**Figure 3. South Somerset District Council
prior to decentralisation**

COUNCIL

|

SEVEN CENTRAL POLICY COMMITTEES

|

CHIEF EXECUTIVE

|

SENIOR OFFICERS

|

SEVEN CHIEF OFFICERS
HEADS OF DEPARTMENT
DEPUTY CHIEF OFFICERS

|

SEVEN DEPARTMENTS

|

SEVEN DELIVERY SYSTEMS

|

CONSUMERS

Politicians have also changed their roles. They spend less time sitting on committees, and more time either in their localities or involved in policy work. As well as a handful of permanent political strategy groups the council creates ad hoc panels to examine policy issues as they come up. Back bench members are encouraged to take a lead on issues of local concern. In the areas, local managers and politicians are used to working together far more closely, almost as a team, in a way that was impossible with a formal committee structure.

The reorganisation has also found new resources within the staff of the council, often by promoting a culture of creative collaboration. The central management of the council is the responsibility of a small executive team, which includes the four area directors. As Mel Usher explained: 'The idea is that they must take responsibility for shaping council policy together because at the end of the day they have to implement it. We had to get away from the idea that there was an executive leadership which was all powerful and to which the buck could be passed.' There is no central housing department and so no chief housing officer in South Somerset to lay down council policy. Instead each of the council's areas has a lead housing officer. These four middle managers combine to create a common approach to policy. Staff within the area offices say they find it much easier to collaborate. Environmental health officers, housing staff, leisure officers are all working in much closer proximity. As a result, joint problem solving and working in cross-functional teams has become far easier.

Perhaps most importantly the changes have created the basis for a more direct relationship between the council and many of its users. As a result, new ideas are more likely to emerge and get translated into practice. For example, most planning decisions are made locally. Planning officers are encouraged to hold meetings on site to encourage local participation. The annual budgets for each area are built from the bottom up through extensive consultation between staff, politicians and users. The community advisers have the leeway to create new outlets for the council's services in libraries and shopping centres. Decentralisation has created the room for experimentation and also provided a way of legitimising greater diversity in provision. This is most obvious in housing. In Chard there is an estate which is run entirely by a 'tenants' democracy' scheme which is almost unique in the UK. In Petherton tenants run a self-build scheme. The council runs a common waiting list with housing associations. All housing alloca- tion decisions are made at area offices. The council has an empty homes strategy and an initiative to provide housing for the young homeless. Tenants' panels are involved in assessing the housing offi- cers' performance and deciding what level of service they want from the council and how much they should pay for it.

Decentralisation is not an end in itself. Structural change is not a guaranteed recipe for entrepreneurship. Yet South Somerset is an outstanding case study of how an hierarchical organisation can devolve power in a way that frees up resources and gives people the confidence to exploit that freedom within a more entrepreneurial culture.

The elements of civic entrepreneurship

The five organisations profiled in this report are exemplars of aspects of civic entrepreneurship. They are all quite different. West Walker is a small school; Thames Valley a large police force; Kirklees is a metropolitan authority; South Somerset is largely rural; Dorset combines a large health authority and hundreds of GPs. These differences are vital. There is no blueprint for entrepreneurship in the public sector. It cannot be set down in a manual. The developments in these five organisations have been heavily influenced by their particular history and culture, the local political setting and even the personalities of those involved. Drawing out the common themes needs to be done with care. Yet policy makers and managers can learn lessons from how entrepreneurship revitalised these organisations.

Focus on outcomes not outputs
All these organisations were inspired by a sense of mission, which focused on producing better outcomes rather than merely producing more output. They were guided by a goal of becoming more effective, not merely more efficient. In most of these cases the process of revitalisation began with a joint effort by political leaders, managers, staff and users to rethink the organisation's goals and purpose. This strategic sense of purpose was not confined to senior managers. They understood that this sense of purpose needed to be shared, ideally from the outset, by politicians, staff and users.

Thames Valley's police's innovative approach to restorative cautioning stemmed from a radical rethinking of policing as the promotion of community safety as well as law enforcement. It is a challenge not just to the practice of policing but its philosophy as well. South Somerset's decentralisation stemmed in part from a philosophy, shared by senior managers and political leaders, that the council should not just provide services but should work closely in alliance with users to help them to help themselves. One of the clearest examples of this focus on outcomes rather than outputs was Norma Redfearn's holistic approach at West Walker Primary School. From the outset she has fostered a rounded understanding of the children's needs and the school's role. Norma Redfearn never defined her goal solely in professional terms of improving attendance and test scores. Her school's focus is broader: to encourage entire families to become more engaged in education.

That wider goal was never just Norma Redfearn's. West Walker's renewal was only possible because parents, teachers and governors created the time and space at the outset in which they thought creatively about what they wanted for the future of the school. This alliance is the basis for the social capital of relationships of trust and mutual support which underpin the school.

Ideally, this focus on outcomes needs to be carried through from goal setting to performance measurement. West Walker's renewal can be measured by the improvements in its attendance record and examination scores. Delivering those was vital to its credibility. But just as important has been its contribution to the social capital of the area, the ability of parents and the community to organise themselves and to become less dependent upon the state. In the longer term, the public sector will only be able to shift its focus from outputs to outcome, from efficiency to effectiveness, with the development of more rounded approaches to measuring performance.

The quality of senior management

Senior managers played a critical role in promoting entrepreneurship in all these organisations. An organisation with committed, entrepreneurial senior managers can innovative despite hindrances. An organisation without entrepreneurial senior managers will find it difficult to innovate, even if it is given a great deal of support and encouragement by national, regional and local politicians. Entrepreneurial senior managers seem to share at least the following characteristics.

- They are prepared to take on vested interests that block change. At both South Somerset and Kirklees senior executives cleared out the top tier of departmental managers to create a more integrated, outward looking management team.
- They have an external focus. They are prepared to learn from outside, whether that is the private sector, international best practice or other public sector organisations. They want to focus their organisations on their clients and the problems they should be seeking to solve.
- They recognise the complexity of the problems their organisation is attempting to tackle and they understand that their capacity to solve the particular problems their organisation faces rests on its ability to forge partnerships with others, to draw on their resources and expertise.
- They understand the limits of their own role. They cannot direct entrepreneurship but they can encourage it, often by being prepared to devolve and delegate power to frontline staff.
- They are good at managing the political and public dimensions of their work, to gain legitimacy for their actions and to renegotiate their mandate. They are not just narrowly focused on process and organisational issues.
- They are extremely persistent. Public sector entrepreneurship is complicated and time consuming. Only the tenacious will succeed. The senior managers profiled in this report have all been in post a long time. Rapid turnover in senior management does not seem conducive to entrepreneurship.
- All these senior managers recognised that they had to become civic entrepreneurs to do their jobs well, helping to forge relationships between staff and clients, managers and political leaders, the organisation and its partners. They were not confined by a professional definition of their task.

Risk management

Entrepreneurship involves taking a risk that a new approach might fail. The café at West Walker Primary School might have been a flop. Thames Valley's restorative justice programme was a gamble with an approach untried in England. South Somerset's decentralisation might have undermined the council's ability to coordinate and integrate its activities. Public sector managers are not encouraged to take risks: they work within legal and financial regimes designed to ensure probity and equity. Public sector auditing and regulation is designed to protect taxpayers' money.

Yet in reality public sector organisations are constantly managing risks. Social services departments are often managing extreme risks to child safety. Care in the community has involved considerable risks. Public sector management is necessarily risk management but public sector managers have to cope with risks different from those facing private sector managers. In the private sector, risks might be measured primarily in financial terms; in the public sector, they are more often measured in terms of public health and well-being. Entrepreneurship adds an extra dimension to risk management in the public sector. Not surprisingly, then, civic entrepreneurs have to be very good at managing the risks perceived to be associated with a new policy or service.

The civic entrepreneurs in this report adopted four main techniques to manage risks. First, risks were shared by bringing together like-minded people and organisations. Forming a partnership is one way to reduce a perceived risk, both financial and political. That stood out in Kirklees' approach to partnerships to build the McAlpine Stadium.

Second, perceived risk can be reduced. Milton Keynes police force reduced the perceived risk of embarking on a new approach to youth crime by showing the costs of sticking with the old approach. As a result the costs of a traditional approach to cautioning and the benefits of a new approach came out more clearly, reducing the perceived risk of making a change.

Third, these organisations were often good at learning from their mistakes. They did not blindly pursue a risky policy when it was not working. They were prepared to go back to find a less risky way of proceeding. When an organisation is taking risk it needs to be much more alert than normal to things going wrong.

Fourth, and perhaps most important, risks must be managed through a political process, which can provide a buffer for managers against public criticism. That is one reason why managers cannot innovate on their own. They need to win political backing for their plans. Entrepreneurship in the public sector is never simply a managerial activity; it is also, always, a political process. That is one reason why private sector models of entrepreneurship do not readily transfer to the public sector.

Building legitimacy

Civic entrepreneurs create a licence to innovate. They are able to renegotiate their mandate in a way that allows them to do a more effective job. Norma Redfearn renegotiated her mandate from teaching children to helping a community to educate itself. Civic entrepreneurship means winning support from politicians, staff and users for the risks that have to be taken in pursuit of a more effective approach, building a consensus around a new strategy. In a world where policy changes were infrequent and public services could stay the same for long periods, legitimacy might have been conferred by periodic elections. But as social and economic change has accelerated so has the need for the public sector to respond by changing what it does. That in turn means that public sector managers and political leaders must engage in a near constant dialogue with staff, users, partners and funders to win support for change. As a result, public sector organisations that wish to develop new services often need to innovate with new, often informal, ways to negotiate consent, through user forums, panels and conferences.

The public sector entrepreneurs in our case studies succeeded because they recognised the need for a time consuming process of winning consent for change. This is not just an external process. Winning the consent of staff is vital. Thames Valley took time to spread restorative cautioning, taking care to build up support within the force. South Somerset's initial attempts to innovate ran into the sand because managers had not involved staff fully enough. Dorset Health Authority went ahead with an innovative approach to involving general practitioners in health planning only after it had cleared the plan with the Department of Health. Significantly, in most of these organisations change rested on a dynamic alliance between senior managers and political leaders. Norma Redfearn could not have succeeded without political support from her governors, who helped her to get around the bureaucratic obstacles placed in her way by the local education authority.

In addition all these organisations maintained their credibility with users because innovation did not distract attention from delivering on the basics of good performance. Norma Redfearn commands credibility in part because her school's performance, judged by national scores, has improved. Dorset Health Authority commands respect in part because its management of the basics of its job has not been harmed by its interest in innovation. In short none of these organisations took their eye off the ball. Their entrepreneurship was more readily accepted because they continued to do the basics well.

Delivering on the ground

Entrepreneurs are actors rather than thinkers. Civic entrepreneurship is a way of acting to reconfigure resources and people in public services to generate greater social value. Entrepreneurship means moving from strategic rethinking into action to make change tangible. The entrepreneurs in this study succeeded because from the outset they understood the need to frame their strategy with an eye on how it would be delivered in practice. West Walker developed a sense of momentum because it first started with tangible, realisable improvements that everyone could benefit from, such as the play-park. Much of the change at South Somerset was evolutionary but landmarks were important, such as the sale of the old head offices in the centre of Yeovil. A great deal of time was spent preparing for change, involving as many people as possible in the discussions. However, once a plan was agreed upon rapid implementation helped to generate a sense of momentum.

Thames Valley, primarily at the urging of middle ranking officers, went slowly enough to learn from mistakes as it introduced its restorative justice programme. It took a decentralised, flexible approach to implementation, which gave local areas the chance to develop their own way to meet a force-wide target of implementing a new approach to cautioning by April 1998. The consultancy led by Ewart Watson played a vital role in implementation. Its staff was drawn from different levels and jobs and so it could talk to staff in the areas at all levels. This allowed it to build up constituencies for change throughout the organisation. It was able to work from the bottom-up as well as the top-down. Restorative justice was underpinned by a new philosophy of policing but the idea of a different kind of caution for first-time offenders was a concrete product not an abstract idea. Officers could understand it much more easily. The consultancy was careful not to oversell the idea as the solution to every problem. They made realistic claims for its effectiveness. They were able to show what benefits it would bring to officers in their day-to-day work.

Working across boundaries

Civic entrepreneurship invariably means working across boundaries, both within and outside the organisation. To create an environment in which her children could learn, Noram Redfearn first needed to make sure they were properly fed and turned up on time. The school stood a better chance of working if its physical and social environment was improved. At West Walker, education is an issue which involved health, the environment, housing, and a social services. The Youth Crime Strategy at Milton Keynes relies on retailers, the police, the probation service and the education system working together. In South Somerset decentralisation has brought council staff together to work in cross-functional teams in area offices, with environmental health, housing and leisure staff often working closely together.

Departmental specialisation is both one of the great strengths and one of the great weaknesses of the public sector. Working across boundaries within and outside organisations has brought several benefits. Cross-functional team working can often help to generate a clearer understanding of a problem and help to unlock the resources needed to tackle it. The Youth Crime Strategy in Milton Keynes relied on a wide range of agencies getting together to jointly address the issue. As a result the complex factors at play in youth crime became clearer as did the kinds of information sharing and joint problem solving needed to tackle the problem.

Kirklees council is an outstanding example of how partnerships with other organisations have not just brought access to resources but to ideas and expertise. The partnerships which helped to create Huddersfield's award winning sports stadium have created a shared capacity to identify and take on new joint projects. These partnerships have created new capabilities for undertaking joint projects which did not previously exist.

Building capacity to create social capital

Civic entrepreneurs know they cannot succeed alone. In all our case study organisations senior managers understood they would only succeed by bringing together people with complementary skills. In most of the organisations entrepreneurship did not depend on an individual but on a team, working entrepreneurially together. Civic entrepreneurs such as Norma Redfearn, Mel Usher and Robert Hughes are strong characters but they recognise how much they depend on the skills of others to succeed. They excel at collaborative leadership, bringing together a team of different but complementary people. There is a pervasive myth that entrepreneurs are heroic individuals. Civic entrepreneurship thrives on collaboration. Civic entrepreneurs understand that they need to develop the capability, skills and knowledge of the people around them and generate greater capacity, that is the amount of effective resources available to achieve their objectives.

This sense of entrepreneurship as creative collaboration extends beyond the staff of an organisation to its users. A striking feature of most of our case studies is that they became more effective by establishing more intimate relationships with their clients, in which users became partly responsible for producing the service they consumed. Norma Redfearn's informal, open style encouraged parents to remain involved with the school. They were not just involved in rethinking the school's purpose and priorities; they are the school's lifeblood. Like members of an educational club, they provide many of its services. South Somerset's decentralisation helped to get users more directly involved in frontline services. The housing service, which is the most decentralised service, has pioneered a variety of schemes to involve tenants more directly in the provision of services. At Thames Valley police, the restorative conferencing approach has brought officers much more intimately into contact with victims of crime. This has helped to create among officers a stronger sense of the people they are serving and among the public a stronger sense of involvement with community safety.

Seeing change as an opportunity

Change in these organisations was not just driven from the inside. Often, the stimulus came from the outside, in the form of a change in government policy. What distinguishes these organisations is their ability to respond creatively to this demand for change. Civic entrepreneurs are visionary opportunists: they have a clear sense of direction but are flexible enough to exploit opportunities as they occur. Civic entrepreneurship crucially involves making a public organisation aware of how it can respond creatively and positively to change. South Somerset's radical plans stemmed in part from the prompting of the Banham review of local government which persuaded the council's leaders to think radically about how to reorganise the authority. Kirklees' partnership to build a new sports stadium was spurred by the Taylor report on safety at football grounds. Norma Redfearn exploited to the full the space for local initiative that was opened up by the local management of schools legislation.

Embedding entrepreneurship

Civic entrepreneurs cannot succeed on their own. Civic entrepreneurship depends on collaboration. It also requires great tenacity and patience. In most of the organisations profiled in this report renewal and innovation took years to take root. Often entrepreneurs in the private sector seem to have a low boredom threshold: they move swiftly from project to project. In the public sector entrepreneurship requires dogged determination as well as charisma and flair. It also requires organisational and cultural change to embed new ways of doing things. West Walker, South Somerset and Kirklees have not simply developed new services, they have devised new forms of organisation. At Thames Valley change has only been possible with a gradual change in the culture. The restorative justice caution will only work if police officers adopt a different attitude towards their work. In all these organisations change was driven by individuals, often several different people.

Yet ultimately, to be sustained it cannot rely on them. Civic entrepreneurship requires organisational and cultural change. This is most evident at South Somerset, where ideas and momentum for change came from different sources at different stages. During the planning stage there were sometimes as many as seventeen groups working on aspects of decentralisation. Managers say this confusion was ultimately creative because of the diversity of ideas that emerged. At different stages senior managers, political leaders and frontline staff provided the momentum to sustain change.

When innovation fails to get off the ground
Our model of how public sector organisations innovate helps to highlight a range of reasons why entrepreneurship often fails to take hold within the public sector.

A focus on outputs rather than outcomes
People are not given the right kind of time and space to rethink the role of the organisation. If there is time to rethink, the effort is focused on the wrong questions: about improving internal processes rather than creating better services. Often when organisations rethink they do not involve the right mix of users and staff alongside senior managers. Rethinking cannot be an ivory tower activity.

Inadequate leadership
The vital role of senior managers is underlined by the way that weaknesses in senior management can hold back an organisation. If there is a lack of leadership it is difficult for an organisation to have a clear strategy. If senior managers are unwilling to take on vested, departmental interests, there will be no integration. If they lack an external orientation, the organisation will find it difficult to learn from the outside and recognise new challenges and needs. If senior managers become too involved in detailed operational issues, they will not pay enough attention to strategy while also crowding out the room for initiative at the frontline.

Risk mismanagement
Often innovations in public sector services fail because they lack public legitimacy or understanding. A good example is the failure of the Kirklees recycling scheme. Entrepreneurship in the public sector can fail not just because of inadequacies in management but because leaders have not done enough to garner legitimacy for change.

Strategy is stillborn
Innovations can fail to take off because the rethinking of how a service

should be designed and delivered is not more than that: thinking. All the organisations in this study closely linked strategic thinking with operational delivery. Civic entrepreneurs lose credibility when they fail to sustain delivery of good performance.

Trapped within boundaries

An organisation can easily fail to recognise the range of other agencies and actors it needs to collaborate with to understand and tackle the complex problems it faces. Solutions do not break down departmental and professional boundaries and budgets. No amount of entrepreneurial dynamism will generate more effective services if the effort remains trapped within organisational boxes. Civic entrepreneurship is about fostering creative collaboration.

Failing to creating new relationships

New services often only work when users are ready for them. An organisation can know how it will implement a brave new plan and yet still fail to deliver a more effective service because it has failed to involve users. Civic entrepreneurship does not just mean creating new services but creating new cooperative relationships with users. Kirklees' recycling scheme failed in part because the council failed to appreciate this. The authority assumed it knew all it needed to know about consumers, when actually it was operating in ignorance.

Conclusions

The public sector is far more innovative than most people imagine. The popular image of the public sector is that it is staffed by time serving, slow moving bureaucrats, happy to hide behind rules and regulations. That caricature is increasingly wide of the mark. There is a huge amount of innovation at the grassroots of the public sector and a great deal of latent entrepreneurship, which is held hostage by the system. Entrepreneurship is always a complex process, which often involves unlocking the tacit side of an organisation, to tap into the uncodified knowledge and ideas of staff. Entrepreneurship cannot be imposed by policy fiat. There is no rule book. There is no blueprint for entrepreneurship or template for innovation. Nevertheless, our study of this group of innovative organisations does suggest that civic entrepreneurship typically has several common ingredients. Lessons can be learned from these best practice, entrepreneurial organisations. Those lessons should inform policy making for the public sector and particularly the creation of a machinery to promote public sector innovation. We need a much more concerted effort to promote and finance, recognise and spread public sector entrepreneurship. It is to the elements of that strategy that we now turn.

Promoting civic entrepreneurship

Civic entrepreneurship will be vital to the remaking of the public sector. Civic entrepreneurs excel at winning support for creative, and sometimes risky, ways to reconfigure resources to deliver improved public services and greater social value. Civic entrepreneurship is not the application of private sector management techniques to public sector organisations. It is simultaneously a political and a managerial activity. Civic entrepreneurship often involves organisational restructuring and individual retraining. But to be successful a civic entrepreneur usually has to do more: renegotiate with politicians, regulators, users and staff an organisation's mandate and sense of purpose.

The innovative, entrepreneurial managers and organisations profiled in this report are creating a new public sector, which is less bureaucratic and more dynamic, comfortable working in partnerships and cross-functional teams. These organisations are creating not just new services but new relationships with the users and communities that they serve. Entrepreneurship in the public sector is not about glitzy marketing, downsizing, re-engineering or borrowing the latest ideas from the private sector. Civic entrepreneurship is about creating a public consensus about how to reconfigure resources, often public and private, to deliver better social outcomes, higher social value and more social capital.

There is a great deal more entrepreneurship in the public sector, especially at its grassroots, than most people imagine. But there is not enough and too much latent entrepreneurship is left untapped. The public sector needs much more effective mechanisms to promote, finance, reward, recognise and spread entrepreneurship. The answers to many of the public sector's problems lie in its own hands. Privatisation, quasi-markets, contracting out and business management methods, can all provide some answers in the right context. But many private sector managers are ill equipped to deal with the complex, time consuming and politicised nature of public sector decision making and accountability.

Yet it is difficult to distil civic entrepreneurship into a replicable form – here are no blueprints or templates. It cannot be delivered by systems or structures, although it can be hindered and encouraged by them. Entrepreneurship and innovation depend on people, the culture of the organisation they work in and the way that the tacit knowledge of staff is brought out.

One of the aims of government policy towards the public sector should be to create spaces in which civic entrepreneurship can flourish. A wide range of factors push and pull, encourage and hinder, entrepreneurship in public sector organisations: national policy, local political leadership, the quality of senior management and the engagement of partners all play a role. What follows are some proposals for how these different players could promote a more entrepreneurial public sector.

National policy
Our case studies showed that national policy can play an important role in spurring and supporting risk taking civic entrepreneurs.

● National policy can help innovation and entrepreneurship by focusing managers on outcomes rather than outputs. Instead of judging the efficiency of an organisation by its throughput – for instance arrest warrants issued by the police, or beds occupied in hospitals – it would be better to focus organisations on the outcomes that they should be seeking: safer communities and improved personal care. How organisations go about delivering these outcomes would then be open to innovation and local discretion. National politics plays a critical role in shaping public debate about the public sector. Politicians are naturally tempted to respond to public worries about the state of public services by trumpeting their efforts to boost outputs and improve efficiency:

more arrests, shorter waiting times. Yet in the long run, creating safer, healthier communities will depend on taking a much wider view of how crime can be reduced and health improved. The more that national politicians can frame the public debate about the public sector's performance in terms of the outcomes society wants, rather than outputs, the more they will create space for innovation and entrepreneurship. This critical role was confirmed by our case studies. In most of the case studies changes to national policy were one spur to the rethinking which eventually led to innovation, for example, the Taylor Report on safety at football grounds spurred Kirklees' approach to partnerships.

- National policy may be one of the few tools strong enough to break the stranglehold that producer interests can exert over public sector organisations. This is perhaps clearest in education, where the combination of centralised target setting and local management of schools has shifted power away from local education authorities and trade unions and towards parents, head teachers and the wider community.

- It is not just a question of policies but of ethos. National politicians play a vital role in validating local initiatives and giving them credence. The innovative initiatives at Thames Valley police and Dorset Health Authority both ran into initial scepticism, but have since gained in credibility because they were seen to run with the grain of national policy.

Just as national policies can enable innovation, they can hinder it in several ways, as the case studies made clear.

- Budgets are often too departmentalised to encourage integrated solutions that involve cooperation between agencies.

- Central regulation of performance targets and spending can be too tight and detailed to allow the flexibility needed for innovation to thrive.

- Public sector managers complain that constant change in the structure and organisation of central government departments makes it difficult for them to know who they are dealing with, on what terms.

Public sector managers who claim that they cannot innovate because central regulation and inflexible budgets weigh them down often use central government as a scapegoat. The innovative organisations profiled in this report show how much can be achieved within the existing framework. Despite that, central government could do more to encourage civic entrepreneurship. Those efforts should follow four themes: to promote, spread, recognise and reward civic entrepreneurship.

Promoting civic entrepreneurship

- Central government can lead by example, by developing a more integrated, holistic, approach to policy making, by pulling together departments into cross-functional teams to address common problems. The Social Exclusion Unit is one example of such integrated policy making unit, which could be applied to other areas such as youth policy and aspects of crime. The evolving cross-departmental approach to spending on under-eight year olds is another. Policy making, target setting and funding can be integrated around particular issues (youth crime); particular client groups (the under-eights) or around particular areas (the creation of health, education and employment zones may help this).
- These experiments with a more integrated approach to policy making could lead to an even more radical overhaul of central policy making. The best councils are well ahead of central government in creating organisations capable of focusing both on strategy and operational delivery. For example, under a Kirklees style approach to central policy making, cabinet members would be given responsibility for strategic issues and social problems, which cut across departments, such as community safety, or the elderly. They would then call upon the resources of various 'back office' departments to solve the problems. This division between strategic responsibility and operational delivery, could help to produce more integrated solutions and reduce turf wars in which cabinet ministers spend large parts of time defending their departmental turf on behalf of their civil servants.

- Policy making to promote innovative, integrated solutions to problems is one thing. Funding these innovative solutions is another. Significantly, the Thames Valley youth crime initiative in Milton Keynes was only possible because of special funding from the Home Office. The cooperative approach to youth crime being pioneered in Milton Keynes could not have been funded by traditional departmental budgets. The government could create an Innovation Fund, to finance projects which cut across departmental budgets. Such a fund could be financed by a levy on all departmental budgets.
- Another approach would be to extend the role of funding by bidding, along the lines of a simpler, less expensive form of City Challenge funding. Central government could specify the range of issues and outcomes it wanted tackled – for instance innovative approaches to youth crime, early release from prison or joint social services and health service initiatives – and seek bids from partnerships created to experiment with new solutions.
- Government could act to remove funding obstacles and boundaries in response to requests from civic entrepreneurs.

Spreading entrepreneurship

- The public sector lacks effective mechanisms to spread the innovative approaches created by civic entrepreneurs. In a competitive market, better products and organisations should drive out worse ones, in theory at least. Takeovers and corporate governance in private sector companies, are partly designed to make sure managers do not underperform. Dynamic regional economies such as Silicon Valley thrive on the rapid translation of bright ideas into entrepreneurial businesses, supported by venture capitalists. None of these mechanisms for developing and spreading entrepreneurship and innovation is perfect. But they are probably more effective than the mechanisms the public sector has at its disposal at the moment. Promoting, recognising and rewarding innovation will not be enough. We also need mechanisms to disseminate and apply the lessons of entrepreneurship more broadly. To create lasting social value on a significant scale we

Regulating for entrepreneurship

Too much top-down, uniform standard setting will inhibit local initiative. Standards based on procedures rather than outputs or outcomes may protect outdated practice. Rigid audit trails and regulations make organisations risk averse. Evaluation and regulatory systems must be fearless in scrutinising how money is spent on the public's behalf and to guarantee safety in critical functions. Yet that focus on probity must be balanced by the need to promote new, more effective, practices. The public sector needs a system of oversight which evaluates not just compliance, but the capacity of organisations to achieve the outcomes they have set for themselves. Audit and regulatory bodies have a vital role in challenging complacency, stimulating new thinking and championing emerging best practice.

This developmental approach to auditing and regulation cannot be directed from the centre. Future developments might include:

- Learning audits, which go beyond assessing success and failure to help schools, hospitals, police forces, to devise alternative strategies to improve performance. Seeing through this process of improvement needs local commitment, knowledge and support. That is a job that regional and local bodies can do far more effectively than experts from Whitehall.
- Extend the use of joint user and peer audits, in which organisations can offer independent evaluation and advice to each other. Most companies draw on ideas and advice from competitors, suppliers, customers and partners as well as paid advisors and non-executive directors. Each public sector organisation should develop a comparable web of contacts to promote learning and adaptation.
- The direct involvement of users in more formal processes of auditing an organisation. In all our case studies users played a vital role in providing a benchmark for organisational purpose and performance. This involvement could be formalised in the form of user's panels, focus groups and advisory panels.

Intermediate bodies

Public sector entrepreneurship is not simply a product of the interaction of national policies, however enlightened, and local management of service delivery. A wide range of intermediate bodies, which stand between central government and the school, police station or housing office, play a vital role. This web of intermediate bodies is complex. Next Step executive agencies are responsible for managing the provision of specific, national services, such as benefits, to achieve government policy. Health authorities are responsible for commissioning health services to meet local needs. Local authorities both commission and provide services. The new governments in Scotland and Wales, the mayor and assembly in London and the new regional agencies all add another layer.

Some of these intermediate bodies play representative roles – as part of political structures – but they also play important roles in managing and supervising public services and in commissioning and allocating resources. The opportunity to develop the entrepreneurial capacity of these intermediate bodies is very significant. The future of local education authorities is under review. Health authorities will play a significant role in the planned reforms to the NHS. The remit of regional government and development agencies is still being debated. Intermediate bodies can enable innovation by acting as collaborative leaders, bringing local practitioners together to share best practice and ideas; creating forums in which local managers can develop a common understanding of a problem; acting as a broker for partnerships with outsiders; protecting a local space for innovation from over regulation from the centre. Equally, these bodies can hinder innovation by second guessing local managers and interfering too directly in issues best left to local management.

The public sector needs a thinking, creative middle layer, able to promote and spread best practice – acting as civic venture capitalists, spotting and then spreading good ideas.

Commissioning for entrepreneurship

The split between purchasers and providers of services is becoming common within the public sector. The role of local authorities, health authorities and perhaps the new regional agencies is moving away from direct service provision to a wider strategic role assessing the needs of a community of users, commissioning services to meet those needs, allocating and coordinating resources accordingly. In many cases, this change of role is the subject of debate as a new consensus is built. For example, the extent of local education authorities' control over resources is disputed. Critics argue that an LEA can control considerable resources that they argue should be destined for schools, while supporters point out that the power of LEAs has declined dramatically in recent years. It is likely that the strategic commissioning role of regional and intermediate bodies will become more not less important. They could encourage entrepreneurship through several roles:

Market making. By changing the purchasing patterns for public services, bringing in new providers for instance, intermediate bodies can engage in active market making to create new sources of supply. For instance, they could help establish new forms of community self-help in housing, health and community safety.

Learning Health and local education authorities can be a conduit for new ideas to come from outside the locality they serve. Often it is difficult for individual head-teachers or hospital managers to raise their heads from their immediate tasks to scan for new ideas. This is a service that intermediate bodies can provide for them. Equally within an area a local education authority should be the forum which helps to create communities of practice and knowledge sharing within professions.

Convening and collaborating. Commissioning bodies have a unique capacity to convene and broker agreements between local providers across agencies and across public and private sectors and to provide collaborative leadership.

Intermediate bodies such as local education authorities and health authorities are often blamed for adding a middle layer of bureaucracy to the public sector. Such a blanket dismissal of the value of these bodies is unfair. Yet they will continue to face pressure to account for the contribution they make to creating social value. One ingredient of that is the role that they create for themselves in promoting and spreading entrepreneurship and innovation.

Local politics

The organisations profiled in this report did not just create new services, they established new ways of involving people in decision making. Service innovation went hand in hand with political innovation in democratic machinery. A creative alliance between political leaders and senior managers was vital in several of our case study organisations. Political leaders play a vital role in helping to create a sense of direction and in managing the risks associated with change, particularly public disquiet and disapproval. They help to confer legitimacy on innovation. In South Somerset District Council, for example, one of the main forces for change was the frustration that the politicians felt with their own role. They saw sitting on committees as a waste of time; they wanted to get stuck into helping solve problems faced by their constituents. Equally the senior managers at South Somerset recognised that their role had a vital political component, to win political support for managerial changes. Politics is a vital and inescapable ingredient of public sector innovation.

Yet politics often stands in the way of innovation. It is difficult for even the best public sector manager to innovate in the face of political instability or opposition. Senior managers in innovative public sector organisations excel at managing the political alliances needed to safeguard their freedom of manoeuvre. To promote more entrepreneurship in the public sector we need to create a local politics which is more conducive to innovation and risk taking.

Traditional departmental committees, overly formal meetings and an almost total separation of political and management responsibility are not conducive to innovation. There are more creative ways of configuring local political processes. The Public Management Foundation's 1996 national survey on the public value of public services, The glue that binds, found that 82 per cent of respondents believed that people who use public services should have more say in how they are run. There has been widespread discussion of the merits of new forms of public participation in decision making – citizens' juries, user panels and local referenda – have been suggested as methods to augment representative democracy. There need be no tension between traditional, or reformed, measures of representative democracy, at local and national level, and new avenues for public involvement at a community or organisational level. However, different techniques for involving the public in decision making are designed to achieve different ends. In education, for example, most parents value involvement in decision making affecting their child. Access to decisions affecting their school matters intensely. Yet most would also recognise that it would be difficult to make decisions about educational priorities across an entire authority using a school based system of parental involvement. Elected mayors may provide more dynamism for local politics, but they may also prove to be more financially conservative than councils. Citizens' juries may prove to be less decisive and ambitious than committed councillors.

The main criteria for judging any democratic reform is whether it expands accountability and involvement in decision making. Yet in addition political reform should be judged for the contribution it could make to a more innovative, value creating public sector. Several questions could be used to assess the potential for political reform to promote public sector entrepreneurship:

- Will it bring in new people to politics?
- Will it encourage more open and informed debate about the purpose of an organisation not just its delivery process?
- Will it take decision makers, physically and culturally, closer to the people?
- Will it involve people more in setting outcomes and auditing effectiveness?
- Will it encourage politicians and managers to challenge the role that they play in service provision?

The growing dependence of the public sector on partnerships with the private sector raises important questions of governance and accountability, which may require novel approaches to community involvement. In a number of innovating public organisations, different approaches are being explored. Learning from these experiments could inform political thinking and management practice.

- One approach might be to test ways of providing users with more direct involvement in decision making about specific services, along the lines of parental involvement in the management of schools. Another possibility would be to pilot experiments with a form of 'democratic service' as a parallel to jury service.

- Another possibility would be to create local versions of the challenge funding being developed in Whitehall. Kirklees council is developing one model in which ward level partnerships between the councillors, community groups and business are being created to bid for money from a council wide community innovation fund. In this example a funding innovation is being used as a lever to spur a political innovation: new ward-level institutions.

- Experiments with more direct forms of user involvement in decision making and alternative forms of democratic accountability, such as the direct election of mayors, should be closely evaluated to assess the contribution they make to civic entrepreneurship.

Public sector management

The least innovative public sector organisations tend to be hierarchical, departmentalised and internally focused. The most innovative organisations are capable of combining, when needed, decentralisation, strategic initiative, integration and external focus. Organisations need an appropriate mix of these qualities. A police force needs a measure of hierarchy and discipline as well as a capacity for decentralisation. Decentralisation for its own sake achieves very little; it needs to be designed to unlock entrepreneurship and to generate new ideas. Decentralisation needs to be matched by a capacity for integration and strategy.

Creating organisations which are capable of delivering higher standards of performance, learning quickly, adapting swiftly and renewing their sense of purpose, is the job of senior managers in the public sector. The most important ingredient in all these innovative organisations profiled in this report was the quality of senior management. These senior managers had a number of characteristics in common: prepared to take risks; frustrated by outdated tradition and departmental baronies; aware of the need to work across departmental boundaries; entered partnerships with outside agencies; ready to devolve operational decision making to the frontline. A new generation of managers is emerging in the public sector. They are frustrated by the public sector of old and prepared to act entrepreneurially. But there are not yet enough of them. We don't just need them at the very top of organisations. We need middle managers with creativity and imagination, with the capacity to work in partnership with users and local people. If there is a single new imperative for public organisations it is to build the capacity of managers to be entrepreneurial. We need a new approach to develop and recognise the value of civic entrepreneurship.

This will involve both 'pushing' and 'pulling' more entrepreneurship from the public sector. By 'pulling' entrepreneurship we mean creating more opportunities for public sector managers to act as entrepreneurs, to unlock the latent entrepreneurship which is held hostage by the system. By 'pushing' we mean building the capacity of public sector managers to be civic entrepreneurs.

Recruitment and selection processes need not only to be fair and open but good at choosing managers with vision and entrepreneurial flair. The job of managing in the public sector is becoming more demanding and complex. Civic entrepreneurs have to articulate a story of where their organisation is headed. Selection procedures need to reflect that: leadership roles should go to people who can lead.

One way to do this is to draw managers from different sources. Public sector managers in the past have been predictably male, white and middle class. Their skills and management style and their ways of seeing the world can be very similar and sometimes create organisational blindspots. By drawing in a greater diversity of people we can create a wider diversity of perspectives and experiences. Women, black managers, people with disabilities, people who have lived abroad, worked in the private or voluntary sector, had divergent career paths, are needed not just to demonstrate a commitment to equal opportunities but to draw on a more diverse pool of knowledge and skills.

Management performance needs to be adjusted as well. Managers need to understand that they will be held accountable for achieving results – not just administering processes. A more rigorous approach to judging performance needs to be matched by a more systematic approach to training and support. Failure should not be a badge of blame but rather should lead to a process of diagnosis, understanding, replanning and trying again. Innovation takes persistence and support.

Public organisations will have to find ways of rewarding performance differently. Promotion and financial rewards should follow entrepreneurial successes but so should non-financial rewards, such as fame and public esteem and opportunities to learn or to lead new projects. One innovation would be to encourage excellent local authority managers to take up more senior positions in Whitehall. Too often the best managers are 'rewarded' by an avalanche of work that kills creativity and creates stress.

Public organisations, strapped for cash, chronically under-invest in developing their managers and staff. The skills and capabilities needed are not easy to build. The capacity to think creatively and strategically, to take risks and to build tricky relationships, are not transmitted through conventional public sector management and training. Conventional management training helps to develop the basic skills needed inside an organisation, but managers need to manage outside relationships as well. Deep technical and professional skills are not enough; they also need broader political and public skills.

Investment in development does not mean spending hundreds of thousands on glossy courses or MBA programmes. Organisations need to create a culture in which learning habitually takes place as part of the work process. In the case studies, opportunities for learning were seized whenever they arose. An organisation can turn most aspects of its work into a learning experience by: encouraging managers to swap jobs, putting together horizontal project teams and learning sets, routinely disseminating learning, sharing development and training with sister organisations. Valuing opportunities to learn is a crucial part of entrepreneurial leadership. Public managers need constantly to expose themselves, and other people in their organisations, to new ideas but then to find opportunities to digest them, test them and find ways to develop them in practice. The most effective development approaches use experiential and action learning, often involve partners from the private and voluntary sectors, as well as other arms of the public sector. Public managers can learn from each other, through best practice networks, buddying systems, benchmarking clubs, shared problem solving groups and learning sets. Perhaps the most important and least used sources of ideas are the public and service users. Working closely with users can generate a fund of ideas and a depth of insight that few training courses can match.

The case for the new public sector

It is still deeply unfashionable to praise the public sector. It has become a convenient whipping-boy, frequently offering itself up for punishment. The state is still largely seen as a slow moving, bureaucratic, hierarchical and unfriendly obstacle to improving living standards. In the 1980s the public sector was repeatedly attacked for falling short of private sector standards. The private sector was seen as efficient, responsive, well managed. The public sector was seen as inefficient, unresponsive and managed in the interests of producers rather than consumers.

The new Labour government marks a sharp break with that approach. It clearly believes that government has a vital role in reviving a sense of civic spirit in Britain. The public sector will be central to the delivery of many of the government's pledges on crime, education, employment and health. Yet that does not amount to an endorsement of the traditional public sector. Far from it. The government clearly wants to promote a role for the central state as a strategic commissioner, enabler and regulator of public services, not necessarily as a funder or provider. It wants a mixed economy of provision, in which the public sector is joined by the voluntary sector, business, social enterprise and new hybrid institutions created through partnerships. There is every sign that it will be impatient with those parts of the public sector unwilling to change fast enough. The public sector will continue to be under pressure, from politicians and the public, to respond more quickly to change and to become more effective.

Civic entrepreneurship is not a panacea in this context. Not all public sector managers can or necessarily need to become civic entrepreneurs. Probity and sound administration are vital components of public management. Public sector renewal can be driven by policy innovation and energetic leadership from the centre. The government's unfolding literacy programme in primary schools is an example of that. Yet civic entrepreneurship must be a central ingredient in the creation of the new public sector that people want. Without a much broader and deeper capacity for entrepreneurship within the public sector, efforts at renewal will prove much more difficult.

Four main themes stand out from this examination of civic entrepreneurship.

First, the public sector can renew itself to become once again a force for modernisation and change in British society. This report highlights just a few of many examples of how the public sector is regenerating itself, creating a new relationship between state and society. There is no necessary reason why the public sector should be left behind or seen as an obstacle for change. The organisations profiled in this report are as impressive as anything the private sector has to offer.

Second, civic entrepreneurship will be a vital part of this renewal. There is within the emerging new public sector a much deeper, wider spirit of entrepreneurship than many people realise. It is not a style of entrepreneurship borrowed from the private sector; that would not work in public sector organisations. Civic entrepreneurship is a distinctive, public sector capacity to win a mandate for innovation and risk-taking to reconfigure resources to deliver higher social value and more social capital. Civic entrepreneurship stands alongside social and business entrepreneurship.

Third, while the public sector will always have much to learn from the private and voluntary sectors, one of the best ways forward is for the public sector to become far better at learning from its own entrepreneurial best-practice. If we could simply find ways getting the mediocre middle in the public sector to learn more swiftly and effectively from the best, public sector performance would improve markedly.

Fourth, while there is more innovation and entrepreneurship in the public sector than many people give it credit for, there is still not enough and would-be entrepreneurs face too many obstacles. To renew the public sector and its role in renewing British society we need a much more effective approach to promoting and funding, rewarding and recognising, disseminating and applying civic entrepreneurship.

For much of the twentieth century the public sector has been associated with modernisation and social improvement. It is only in the last two and a half decades that it has become publicly associated with decline and under-achievement. Despite two decades of cuts and restructuring the public sector remains central to British society and touches most people's lives. It can once again become a source of renewal in British society: to do so, it must untap the spirit of civic entrepreneurship within it.